REMARKS

ON

CAVALRY.

Light Dragoon Officer

REMARKS

ON

CAVALRY;

BY THE PRUSSIAN MAJOR GENERAL OF HUSSARS,

WARNERY.

TRANSLATED FROM THE ORIGINAL.

WITH AN INTRODUCTION BY
BRENT NOSWORTHY

CONSTABLE · LONDON

First published in Great Britain 1798
This edition published 1997 by Constable and Company Limited
3 The Lanchesters, 162 Fulham Palace Road, London W6 9ER
ISBN 0 09 477320 3
Printed in Great Britain by
St Edmundsbury Press Ltd, Bury St Edmunds, Suffolk

A CIP catalogue record for this book is available from the British Library

TO

FIELD MARSHAL

His Royal Highnefs the Duke of York,

COMMANDER IN CHIEF,

&c. &c. &c.

SIR,

THE universal admiration of your Royal Highnesses transcendant virtues, renders every attempt
at panegyrick in this place superfluous; it remains
therefore only to observe, that every undertaking
which has had for its object, the promotion of

the

the true principles of military science, has been constantly honoured with your Royal Highnesses approbation; should this hasty translation experience similar good fortune, the highest ambition of the Translator will be amply gratified.

I have the honor to be,

With most profound respect

And submission,

Your ROYAL HIGHNESS's

Most obedient

Humble servant,

London, March, 1798.

G. F. KOEHLER,
Lieut. Col. &c.

P R E F A C E.

THE high eftimation in which the following remarks have been conftantly held by feveral of the firft cavalry officers, not only in our fervice, but in Europe in general, was the confideration which firft induced the tranflator, as a military ftudy, to undertake a tranflation of it;* and afterwards, by the advice and recommendation

.of

* Next to martial exercifes, nothing conduces more to roufe the courage of a foldier, or "to make him better acquainted with the military art, than his employing the leifure of . "winter quarters, and the many irkfome hours fpent in garrifon, in the ftudy of fuch "fciences as are moft commendable and ufeful." Buonamici's Preface, Wars of Italy, "Book I.

"None, I am perfuaded, will be fo unreafonable, as to blame me for employing the "little leifure a foldier can find from the duties of his profeffion, in ftudy, reading, or "even writing, provided the fubject be not incompatible with the character he fuftains, "as that of this tranflation certainly is not." Ibid.

feveral of his friends, to lay it before the public, more efpecially as the original has been fome time out of print, and not to be procured, even in Lublin, the place where it was firft publifhed.

Like all other things founded upon folid and permanent principles, its reputation has been fo far from diminifhing, by the lapfe of time, (being originally publifhed in 1781) that it has on the contrary, only become the more approved in proportion, as it was more generally known. It is the work of a real officer of cavalry, who took the greateft delight in his profeffion, and diftinguifhed himfelf very much in it. It would be an improper liberty to quote the authority of thofe excellent and diftinguifhed officers of cavalry, in confequence of whofe recommendation the prefent tranflation was put to the prefs; but it will be permitted to obferve that it was not the leaft prevailing motive that the late Lord Heathfield, whofe aid de camp the tranf- lator had the honor to be, always mentioned the original with peculiar approbation, as well as in general all the other works of the fame author : Thefe confiderations, it is prefumed, will be deemed a fufficient apology for the appearance of the prefent tranflation. It now only remains to folicit the indulgence of the candid reader, with regard to the ftile, to admit the importance of the fubjeft as an excufe for the inaccuracies of the compofition; if the fenfe of the original has been faithfully rendered, it is hoped that the graces of rhetoric will not be expefted in this hafty military fketch.

With

'With regard to the plates, it was long time a doubt whether to add them to the work or not, from the difficulty, time and expence, which it would require to procure proper engravings of the figures to be reprefented; but the tranflator having by him feveral hafty fketches which feemed to correfpond very well with the work, and which he was advifed to add to it, if poffible, conceived it would be more acceptable to have them even in their prefent rough and unfinifhed form, than to be totally without them, more particularly as they are not intended as an embellifhment: but merely as illuftrations and explanations of the various fpecies of cavalry employed in the different nations in Europe. It will therefore not be expeded, nor is it intended, that they fhould in any manner, reprefent or explain the different exercifes of the carbine, fwords, management of the horfes, &c. this would require a work peculiarly apropriated to that purpofe, and totally different from the prefent, and was rendered the more impradicable and improper in the prefent work, from the fketches reprefenting different nations, or different natures of troops in the fame nation, each of which would have different manners of performing their exercife, and therefore rendered impoffible to accomplifh any regular or fyftematical reprefentation of it, and it was thought more advifable not to attempt what would be inconfiftent, and therefore improper. Thofe prints are therefore only intended to give an idea of the various natures of cavalry, in the European and other armies, fo far as the tranflator had it in his power, in the prefent moment, to perform it.

c

It

It was intended likewife to have added fome more remarks applicable to the fervice of cavalry, from the other excellent works of the fame author: but not to procraftinate the prefent work, it was deemed more expedient to publifh this feparate, and afterwards, if that fhould appear defirable, to make a diftinct work of them; or to ftimulate fome other perfon more competent to the undertaking to perform it; as it is conceived that every light thrown upon the fubject of cavalry, by fo excellent an author, who has joined practice to theory, and inculcates nothing but what he has actually feen performed, or bore a part in himfelf, cannot fail of being acceptable to every military reader; particularly officers of cavalry.

The following defcription of the light cavalry, employed in the army of the famous Kouli Khan, appeared to be too apropos to the prefent fubject to be omitted.

The Perfian horfes are large, and the horfemen commonly well made; they wear great muftaches, and have, inftead of a turban, a fquare bonnet a foot and a half high, covered with goats or tygers fkins, that has the hair on it. To this turban is fixed a plate of bended iron, a foot long, with which they ward off the blows of fabres, by certain motions of the head, which they make with great agility; their drefs, which is red, green, or yellow, is wide and fhort, with large fleeves; they have under this, a kind of fhift, open on the breaft, and ufe drawers, and leather boots. As for their arms, they confift of

a firelock,

a firelock, a hatchet a fabre, and a buckler. Thefe horfemen, with their accoutrements, which they know to be formidable to their enemies, marched boldly to them, as being fure of the victory. They attacked them wherever they met them, and fometimes purfued until they came under the battery of cannon. In feveral of thofe fallies, during fifteen days, Mohamed Schah loft above 50,000 men.

Tranflation, M. L. Abbé Lambert, vol. II. page 319.

Thamas Kouli Khan obferved it as a maxim never to feparate his troops, left fome detachment being beaten, the reft might be dif-pirited by that means. He ufed to fay that the victorious, by flow marches, come up to the enemy, fly as faft as he can.—*page* 209, vol. II.

He fet out with an army of no more than 20,000 men; there were only 12,000 of thefe regular troops, who wore coats of mail, covered with plates of brafs; the reft were only valets, and young perfons, whom they call Jelim, that is orphans, who ferve but for little elfe than to ruin the country through which the enemy paffes.

Tranflation M. L. Abbé Lambert, page 216, vol. II.

CONTENTS.

d   XI.   Of

INTRO-

INTRODUCTION.

AMONGST the great variety of military books which have hitherto been publifhed, very few throw any new light upon the fervice of cavalry; a proof that the fervice of this nature of troops has never been fufficiently underftood, and that it requires many talents, and military qualities, to become a great officer in it. It is not to be doubted, that for feveral centuries paft, cavalry has very much degenerated, and it is only within thefe few years that its juft principles have began to be revived and applied, and which promifes fair, foon to reftore it to its ancient luftre, and pre-eminence. Formerly cavalry conftituted the principal ftrength of an army, and all perfons of diftinction were ambitious to ferve in it; but the French Gens d'Arms having been frequently routed and difperfed, and at length totally defeated by the Swifs infantry, particularly at the battle of Novarre, feemed to eftablifh a decided fuperiority of that arm over cavalry, and caufed infantry, from that epocha, to be prefered, and cavalry confequently in European armies, to be neglected; and from that time, until the reign of

Frederick

Frederick II. cavalry, thus degenerated and neglected, rendered few services equal to what they had before been accustomed to perform, and it will appear in the course of the following remarks, that the very erroneous principles adopted by them, rendered their mode of fighting almost contemptible.

Several respectable military authors appear to have been entirely unacquainted with the importance, and advantage, of the services which might be rendered by that species of troops. Quinci, who has so much and so ill written, makes the exercise of cavalry consist solely in the caracol or wheeling in line, Birac, who is instructive enough in what relates to parties, detachments, and the service of light cavalry, in the petit Guerre, mentions it as an important consideration, that the trooper should be provided with boots and a cloak, a proof that they were in his time without them. Puifegur, who has treated most elaborately upon cavalry, has shewn that he was much less acquainted with that service than is required of a Subaltern officer amongst the Pruffians.

Folard confiders cavalry as almost a ufelefs and inconvenient piece of furniture; it was however in his time, that the great Elector, Frederic William, with his cavalry alone, defeated the whole Swedish army, at Ferbelin; and without cavalry, what advantage could Frederic have reaped from all his victories? It was his cavalry which in the two last wars rendered him the most important services, particularly at Strigau, Sohr, and Keffelfdorf, where they decided the fate of the action, by the impetuofity and courage of their charge; his Huffars did the fame at Prague; the affair of Rofbach, was decided by a few fquadrons, and Seydlitz, with cavalry alone, retrieved the fortune of the day, at

Zornfdorf:

Zornfdorf; and faved the remainder of the infantry, at Hochkirk, &c.
there are, however, not wanting, perfons, who, without being well
informed, pretend that the Pruffian cavalry is not to be ranked amongft
the beft. It is not to be denied that they have been repulfed, and that
fometimes, even after a fuccefsful charge; but it muft be recollected,
that an accident, a wing out flanked, a ditch, a cloud of duft, an appel
or rally imprudently founded; a fudden and inconfiderate movement,
the fire of cannon, at the inftant of the commencement of the charge,
might happen to throw the beft cavalry, for an inftant, into diforder:
befides, our cavalry (the Pruffian) was every where, by half their
number, inferior to that of their enemies, and reduced to the neceffity
of manœuvring in two ranks; but what, in my opinion, contributed
moft towards this want of fuccefs, whenever that was the cafe, was
its charging en murialle, or without intervals, or at leaft with them too
fmall: the King would have it fo; but whenever the Generals were
at liberty to leave reafonable intervals, it was always fuccefsful; this
article will be hereafter more fully difcuffed. It is however inconteft-
able, that moft of the regiments have performed brilliant actions: and
particularly the Huffars, under the command of General Seydlitz,
who was, for fo long time, their chief. This great man adopted, and
introduced fuch alterations, and improvements, as entirely changed
the nature of the fervice of cavalry in general: but more particularly
of the Huffars; his fyftem was peculiar to himfelf, and in which, he
admitted nothing but the ufeful; and it is impoffible to carry the perfection and fuperiority of that arm, beyond what he has done. The
conftitution of the Pruffian army renders it however very difficult to
inftruct and train a foldier in it, to that perfection which is required by
the reglement; half the foldiers being on furlough ten months in the
year, they, during that time, forget what they had before been in-

e   ftructed

ftructed in, and at the time of their rejoining, preparatory to the reviews, they are almoft as ignorant as recruits; an inconvenience which does not happen in thofe fervices where this œconomical arrangement is not eftablifhed, and where the foldier can be maintained in continual exercife.

It is the fyftem of the General before mentioned, which is intended to be obferved in thefe remarks; the principles which he eftablifhed, are of that General and permanent nature, as to be applicable to every defcription of cavalry, and enable each to act with the other, as occafion might require, or to perform feparately and alone, the fervice proper to each; the cuiraffiers with the Huffars, fuplenefs, activity, order, attack, difperfe, appel, rallying, all is fimplified and equalifed amongft them. It was Seydlitz, who, after the peace of Drefden, began to unnumb and quicken the activity of the Huffars, to which nature of troops he was extremely partial; and they have hitherto been the only troops of that defcription which have been trained to perform the double fervice of regular cavalry and Huffars; except the Ruffians, who have began in this to imitate them. The Pruffian Huffars have charged in clofe fquadron, equal to the beft cavalry of any nation; and what have they not performed in detachments, and the Petit Guerre? This advantage can proceed only from the manner in which they are trained and exercifed: for the troopers* in general confift of German Peafants, and are for the moft part taken by force, from the plough, and their homes; almoft all the officers are educated in their regiments, and except their ordinary exercife, and manœuvres, they learn very little in their garrifons

* In the courfe of this work, all the foldiers who are formed into troops, are called troopers, though that denomination is ufually applied to heavy troopers only.

rifons and quarters; and it is very rare to find amongft them, men of polite education and manners. Their ideas in general does not extend beyond their profeffion: but it muft be confeffed, that they acquire a certain routine, which enables them to decide exceedingly well upon the moft critical occafions, which can occur in actual fervice. Since Seydlitz has commanded the cavalry, the cane has very properly been almoft forgot; every individual trooper ought to be perfonally brave, and to be animated with that noble ambition, which too much pains cannot be taken to infpire him with; to effect which, in fome fervices, they are treated with particular refpect; without this powerful ftimulus they can find a thoufand pretexts to evade doing their duty in prefence of the enemy, and as many excufes are always ready; they can lay the blame upon their horfes; whereas in the infantry it is much eafier to oblige men to preferve their ranks and files, and to fire: if not to advance to the charge with the bayonet.

If a foldier, whether on foot, or on horfeback, is not animated with ambition, if he has not that patriotick fpirit, (the diftinguifhing characteriftick of the Englifh, and the Ruffians) he cannot be depended upon on any occafion where it is not fufficient to act mechanically; but where perfonal bravery is likewife requifite. The Pruffians have not fucceeded to form their cavalry to its prefent perfection, without great labour and perfeverance; many nations have much greater facility of forming theirs the fame, efpecially thofe where the fyftem of furloughs is not adopted.

It was formerly imagined that a Huffar could not be good, unlefs he was an Hungarian; experience has however proved this to be an error, amongft the Pruffian Huffars there are few, if any, of that

nation;

nation; by perfeverance and labour, men may be brought to perform whatever can be required of them, provided it does not exceed human capacity.

The ordinary exercifes of cavalry will not be much touched upon, in the following remarks, there being already books which fully treat upon that fubject; a very different one from what is denominated manœuvers. Exercife forms the foldier, renders a troop compact and difembarraffed in its movements: it confifts principally in the different manners of breaking into column, of re-forming into line, of marching, and all the evolutions of the parade, rather than what is properly called manœuvres. Military exercife is every where almoft fimilar, it is only neceffary to obferve, that it be performed with fpirit, and accuracy, and as fhort as poffible; that it might not require too much time, nor occafion unneceffary fatigue to the men or horfes. The Ruffians have formed, of the leaft efteemed of their Coffacks, regiments of Huffars, who have made themfelves to be refpected by the Turks, which is certainly faying a great deal in their favour, and fhews what might be done by fyftem and method.

Exercife is properly only a preparation for the manœuvres, and as foon as a foldier is perfect in the former, he fhould be inftructed in the other.

It is much to be regretted that a nation like Poland*, which poffeffes all that can be required to form excellent troops, as well infantry

as

* It is perhaps not neceffary to obferve, that the original of this Work was publifhed previous to the change which has taken place in that country.

as cavalry, cannot maintain a number fufficient to eftablifh order, fupport the impartial diftribution of juftice, and the internal regulations of
police; but thofe who are acquainted with the form of that govern-
ment know that the King, who commands only the four regiments of
guards, has it not in his power. Prince Adam Czartoryfki does every
thing he can to reftore the military reputation of his country to
its ancient fplendour, and with that intention has already expended
very confiderable fums of money; even the diflocation of Poland did not
difcourage him from his noble and patriotical refolution.

It is curious to remark the fluctuations of military reputation, in
the different fervices of Europe. Formerly the Spanifh infantry
were the moft efteemed, and now, perhaps without reafon, their
cavalry is preferred. In fome wars, the Auftrian cavalry has not
diftinguifhed itfelf fo much as their infantry. The Hungarians were
fuppofed to be proper for cavalry, or Huffars only; at prefent their
infantry does not give place to that of any other nation.

And it might be juftly affirmed without prepoffeffion or prejudice, that
towards the end of the laft war, the King of Pruffia received more de-
ciffive fervices from his cavalry than his infantry; although on his
coming to the throne, the latter feemed to be fuperior to that of every
other nation.

According to Philip de Comines, the Spaniards, in his time, had
large horfes proper for the Gens d'Arms, or heavy horfe: thofe of the
Englifh, on the contrary, were fo weak, as to be fcarcely capable of
being mounted by the archers; and in effect, in the battles between the
Stuarts, and the Lancafters, all, even the Kings themfelves, were obliged

f

to

to fight on foot; at prefent we fee the race of horfes, in each of thefe nations, entirely changed. Two hundred years paft, the Kings of France had fcarcely any national infantry, and had recourfe to the Swifs, the Germans, and even to the Italians for them; at prefent the French infantry is fuppofed to be fuperior to the cavalry of the fame nation: and in what fmall eftimation was the Hungarian infantry held? It was only in the reign of the Emperor Charles VI. that they began to be employed, and they are now fuppofed to be as firm, and fteady, as any troops in the world.

It is proper to obferve that thefe remarks were not written with the intention of their being rendered public, but folely for the inftruction of fome young perfons of the firft diftinction, deftined for the fervice of cavalry.

INTRODUCTION
By Brent Nosworthy

It seems only natural that many details about the lives of such notable Prussian military commanders as Seydlitz, Schwerin and Zieten have been recorded and passed down to posterity but, strangely, few details have survived about Karl Emanuel von Warnery. We do know that Warnery, born in 1719, was of Walloon descent and that he entered the Prussian service as a young man, but little is known about the early part of his career. Whether through influence or obvious talent, Warnery quickly rose in rank and by 1745 had been appointed to *Oberstlieutenant* with the Puttkamer Hussars. Regardless of the reasons for his quick promotion, Warnery immediately displayed cool judgement, *coup d'oeil* and steel nerves on the battlefield.

Unusually analytical and articulate as he was, it is not surprising that our hussar was able to befriend such influential officers as Seydlitz, with whom he worked successfully on the battlefield. Warnery participated in Seydlitz' successful charge during an action at Landshut,

Silesia (1745) after they had led their regiments through a gap in the front line created by a regiment less alive to the opportunity. They combined again to defeat an Austrian rear guard commanded by Count Burghauson near Zittau the same year.

By the opening of the Seven Years' War, Warnery had been promoted to Colonel of the 3rd Hussars and, according to the *Militar-Wochenblatt* (no. 57), Warnery had the honor of firing the first shot of this new round of hostilities. Warnery's quick eye and firm resolve continued to outmatch his opponents. Leading 450 hussars at Schandau in 1756, he managed to destroy a regiment of Austrian grendadiers commanded by then Lieutenant-Colonel Loudon. Probably his most notable success, however, came during the Battle of Prague. Warnery noticed a defect in the Prussian cavalry dispositions on the extreme left which he brought to General Norman's attention. The latter, in command of the Prussian second line of cavalry on that flank, refused to do anything about it, claiming he lacked sufficient authority. Disregarding the normal chain of command, Warnery ordered his own regiment to move out to the left to prevent the Austrians under General Haddick from outflanking them. Warnery then led a charge which effectively neutralized the immediate Austrian cavalry threat in that area. After the battle Warnery was congratulated by Frederick himself.

In the 1770s, General Warnery decided to turn to the more theoretical side of his profession and write campaign studies, as well as more military scientific works. He became a prolific writer and during the next eighteen years his books were published in the Germanies, France, Great Britain, Holland and Poland, which suggests he had developed a strong readership among the officers in all the major western European armies of the period.

His first work, *Remarques sur le militaire des turcs et sur la façon de les combattre*, a systematic examination of the Turkish armies, was a long overdue work that filled a noticeable gap in western European military science. First published in Leipzig in 1770, it was so popular that a second edition was released the very next year in Breslau. One of Warnery's rare qualities was that he was as much at home among the intellectual as he was among the practical. His second publication, *Commentaires sur les commentaires du Comte Turpin sur Montecuculi* (Breslau, 1777–79) was an exegesis of Turpin de Crissé's seminal analysis of the great commander, Montecuculi.

Warnery's next work was much more encyclopedic. The *Anecdotes et pensées historiques et militaires* sought to examine a number of incidents that occurred during the wars of the eighteenth century with a view to evaluating the efficacy of current military and tactical practices. Though penned in 1774, it was only published in Halle in 1781. The same year saw the publication of what would prove to be Warnery's most popular and enduring work, *Remarques sur cavalerie*. Originally published in French at Lubin, a German translation appeared the next year at Leipzig. These were Warnery's most productive years and a succession of other works soon followed: *Malange de remarques, sur-tout sur César* (Warsaw, 1782); *Remarques sur plusiers auteurs militaires et autres* (Lubin, 1783); *Des Herrn Generalmajor von Warnery Samltliche Schriften* (Hanover, date unknown); and *Campagnes de Frédric II, roi de Prusse, de 1756 à 1762* (Amsterdam, 1788). Unfortunately for students of military history, General Warnery's scholarly career was cut short with his death in 1789.

When Warnery first sat down to write in the mid-1770s, it must have appeared that most of the century's great military scientific works had already been written. The British tactician Humphrey Bland had long since unveiled his comprehensive treatise on infantry tactics which he scrupulously kept up to date with periodic revised editions for almost forty years. Possibly to compensate for two generations of martial mediocrity, France in particular enjoyed a golden age of military writing and the years that separated the treaties of Utrecht and Paris (1713–63) witnessed the publication of a number of seminal works. The Chevalier Folard had published *Nouvelles découvertes sur la guerre* and *Histoire de Polybe*, which challenged the prevalent linear tactical system. On the traditionalist side, Maréchal Puységur published his two-volume *Art de la guerre par principes et par règles*, which, although published in 1748, described French military art from Turenne's time to the War of the Polish Succession. Count Lancelot Turpin de Crisse's three-volume work, *An Essay on the Art of War*, the original French edition of which appeared in 1754, proved to be a timely piece that conveniently prepared officers for the intricacies of the daily campaign operations they would soon encounter in the Seven Years' War. Others, such as the *Traité de la petite guerre*, were a discussion of partisan warfare.

Despite this seeming plethora of in-depth works on the military art, there was still lacking a comprehensive treatment of cavalry doctrine and practice. Not only did all of the works above pay scant attention to the cavalry, Warnery also felt that what did exist had largely been written either by infantrymen or by theoreticians with little or no cavalry experience in the field. To compound the problem, nothing had been written to reflect the profound changes in cavalry practice that had been effected by the Prussians in the 1740–63 period.

The results of Warnery's efforts was a masterpiece, arguably one of the most distinctive works produced in a century of great military writing. There are a number of reasons for the work's importance, other than being simply a fascinating book. More than any other single work, *Remarks on Cavalry* provides moderns with a glimpse of what it was like to be a cavalry officer, describing the most important techniques and tactical procedures, as well as how the young officer was to set about mastering these. Just as importantly, however, the work also chronicles the forces of change at work within the Prussian cavalry during the mid-eighteenth century. The foundation of Napoleonic cavalry doctrine was largely forged by Frederick, Seydlitz and other influential Prussian cavalry officers. So many of the details provided in this work shed light on a number of long-term tactical developments, rather than simply describing a local practice during a narrow time frame.

Since it is unreasonable to assume that all readers are intimately conversant with the nuances of eighteenth-century cavalry tactics, a few words of background are in order. Moderns tend to assume, albeit unconsciously, that a gradual evolution is constantly underway, so that the tactical and combat methods of the War of Polish Succession are slightly different from those that had been used during the Great Northern War, and that those used during the War of Austrian Succession have developed since 1734–36. Contrary to our expectations, however, the methods of resolving combat on the European battlefield remained much the same between 1715 and 1740. In other words, when the Austrians embarked on the war that had been imposed upon them by the ambitious new Prussian king in 1740, their manuals of arms, formations and tactical procedures were almost identical to those used by their fathers during the War of Spanish Succession nearly thirty years previously. Within sixteen years, however, a new style of warfare would emerge, one which placed much greater importance on manoeuvre and grand tactical finesse, and which would culminate in Frederick's triumphant victories at Leuthen and Rossback.

Ironically, the seeds of these changes would ultimately stem from a seemingly trivial practice, which in itself was actually detrimental. This, of course, was Frederick Wilhelm's mania for constant ceremonial-style drilling. Whether because of some eastern influence or the indirect result of Maurice de Saxe's views about the potential importance of cadence marching, this practice was adopted by the Prussian infantry sometime during the late 1730s. This newly acquired talent for more organized and controlled marching was to prove a watershed event, facilitating, even prompting, numerous other innovations that had been hitherto impossible, if not literally inconceivable.

Up until this time, prior to a set-piece action, the long columns had to approach the intended position from the rear. Then, they would turn 90 degrees, marching across the battlefield, usually from left to right, before finally quarter-wheeling into line. This was an extremely time consuming process that also severely restricted the commander's grand tactical options just prior to and during the first phases of a battle. Sometime during the 1740s, probably in the latter stages of the Second Silesian War, the Prussian tacticians devised the *traversier-schritt* method of forming line. This was a cumbersome manoeuvre requiring the men in an open-order column to perform a prance-like step as they marched obliquely from the column into line. In 1748, a slightly modified version appeared which reduced the angle of the oblique march that had to be performed during this manoeuvre. Each tier in the column wheeled about 20 to 25 degrees and then marched where line was to be formed. Yet a third method of 'deploying' into line was introduced in 1752. This was the *en tiroir* manoeuvre, that is deployment by 'square movements.' These were all techniques to deploy from column to line. A number of other manoeuvres which could be described as the inverse of these were devised to 'ploy' from line to column.

The new deployment manoeuvres were not intended to replace the traditional processional methods that had been used to deploy entire armies. Rather, they had been designed to allow individual battalions and regiments to form line quickly in certain critical but isolated situations. They also allowed battalions in an extended line to 'ploy' momentarily back into column in order to skirt round whatever obstacles they might encounter, such as ponds, morasses, etc. Once past, they would use the manoeuvres to quickly 'deploy' back into line.

All of these developments affected the Prussian infantry arm, but it is not at all obvious why they had so much impact on the way Prussian and, later, nearly all European cavalry would be handled. Prior to the advent of the Prussian manoeuvre system, cavalry had been severely limited in its scope of action on the battlefield, regardless of the tactics it used to charge the enemy or fight. Once deployed, except for extenuating circumstances, it was difficult for a cavalry formation to do anything but to advance straight ahead.

All this would change with the introduction of the new-style manoeuvres which were applied to cavalry and infantry almost simultaneously. True, it was impossible to apply cadenced marching to the horse's movements. What was possible, however, was to take the geometrical and procedural concepts upon which each infantry manoeuvre was based and create an equestrian equivalent. Let us take as an example the quarter-wheel slightly to the left, advance straight ahead, and then quarter wheel slightly to the right method of forming line. This manoeuvre required the unit to be broken down into a number of subunits, such as a platoon or division of the battalion. Each subunit then performed a series of geometrical movements in a prearranged order. The cavalry equivalent required the same type of general steps in the manoeuvre, even though the way the horse performed a particular step in the process might be physically different from the way it was performed by an infantryman.

There was a second thread of tactical developments that, together with the above manoeuvres, would transform the awkward, overly heavy cavalry under Frederick William into the most powerful and successful cavalry of the epoch. This was the creation of an entirely new charge doctrine, which would give the Prussian cavalry a decisive advantage over its opponents. In 1740, the Prussian cavalry, burdened by excessively large men, advanced to the attack often at only a fast walk. The dismal results were predictable. Frederick realized that, if his cavalry arm was ever to be successful, it must combine two important ingredients during the last moments of the charge: speed and cohesiveness. The first steps in this direction were modest. Unsuitable men were replaced and in 1741 the Prussian cavalry was ordered to charge the last thirty paces at the gallop. This was increased to 100 paces in March 1742 and a full 200 paces in July 1744.

The ability to quickly perform sophisticated manoeuvres close to the enemy, as well as the introduction of a more effective charge doctrine, ultimately converted the Prussian cavalry into the premier cavalry in western Europe. In the work that follows Warnery not only provides many of the details of the new doctrine but how the transition came above in the first place. Nowhere else is there such a detailed description of the Prussian cavalry column of attack. As much as one scours Frederick's own writings, one will not find such a vivid explanation of the new charge doctrine, its effectiveness or why it was developed.

Although very much less obvious, there is a second reason why *Remarks on Cavalry* is a 'must read' for anyone seriously interested in military history/science during either the linear or Napoleonic periods. Although *Remarks on Cavalry* might conform to a modern reader's expectations of what a comprehensive discussion of military art should include, it represented a fundamental departure from the manner in which military scientific works had been treated up to that point. Like the writings of Frederick the Great, Warnery's work attained a new, more sophisticated level of analysis and treatment. In terms of the expositional style, the methodology embraced, and the entire underlying philosophical approach, Warnery's work was literally fifty to sixty years ahead of its time. Only after the conclusion of the Napoleonic Wars would comparable works be penned by De Brack, Bugeaud and Nolan. It was access to this new more powerful conceptual approach to the systematic study of warfare that explained the advantage that Frederick, his staff and generals enjoyed over their contemporaries.

That is not to say there was a shortage of material among the existing body of military scientific work. When the full spectrum of military treatises is considered, one can eventually find a treatment of almost any subject. In LeBlond's *Element de Tactique* one can extract the best explanation of the differences between the Dutch fire by platoons and the French *feu de rangs* (fire by ranks), why each was used and their respective strengths and weaknesses. Puységur gives the most comprehensive description of what it was like to deploy into line and ploy back into column before the advent of cadenced marching. Turpin de Crissé is a master at explaining what precautions were required to defend a column of march as it wended its way through the countryside during the day-to-day operations of a campaign and conversely how to successfully attack the opponent's column. The problem is that most of the mid-eighteenth-century military writers limited the great bulk of their treatment to one or two main topics and only provided well-hidden fragments of information about others. LeBlond's work is probably the best example. One has to plod through

500 pages of a theoretical system of infantry manoeuvres that was never used in practice before one discovers his wonderful discussion of the pragmatic reasons underlying the various fire systems then in use.

The other problem with what had by then become the traditional approach to military writing was that, for the most part, it limited itself to the purely mechanistic dimension of the military art. In works written prior to 1750 one finds numerous descriptions of manual of arms, as well as how to form the troops into line at the beginning of the exercise. Starting in the early 1750s these increasingly are accompanied by descriptions of the new manoeuvering systems then being introduced. What is so noticeably absent in these works, however, is discussion about why a practice was adopted and the difference between what was rehearsed on the parade ground and what was actually done on the battlefield. The reasons for this were twofold: the concept of 'tactics' as it then existed, and what was considered to be the self-conscious purpose of military writing. In 1750, 'tactics' was a newly emerging concept. Originally, it referred only to the methods of bringing troops on to the battlefield. Soon, it was also applied to the methods of moving troops after the engagement had begun, and gradually came to define the movement and use of troops to secure a localized advantage over the enemy.

Thinking about the Prussian army during the 1740–63 period, one is likely to conjure up an image of highly-trained, well-lead soldiers who had access to an assortment of new tactics and methods. In its own way, this is accurate enough. However, at the heart of this innovation was something that has long been overlooked. The new Prussian methods did not come about simply as a result of one man's genius. Rather, they arose because of a new relationship between the military authorities and the subject matter under dissection. As one scours Warnery's *Remarks on Cavalry* and Frederick the Great's writings one sees that, to a then unheard of degree, Prussian military authorities discussed not only what they were to do, but the reasons why one method was effective and another was not. Many examples can be found, such as the creation of the echelon formation, etc., where Frederick and his generals turned to what had just occurred on the battlefield for a new source of inspiration. This was the opposite of the tendencies in other military circles, where emphasis was placed on either the traditional approach or some alternative *theoretical* system. When one examines Folard or LeBlonde's works, for example, one finds the authors proffering mathematical-like systems, the military equivalent of post-Cartesian idealism then so prevalent in philosophical treatises. Frederick, Warnery and the other Prussian military authorities were completely pragmatic. Rather than looking at the theoretical and attempt to apply it in practice, they were rooted in what happened on the battlefield and what was demonstrated to work, need improvement or be discarded as impractical.

By shifting the focus in this way to what tended to occur on the battlefield, Frederick and his tacticians, even if only unconsciously, became aware of what today would be referred to as the 'psychological' dimension of warfare, i.e. those factors that tend to act upon the troops to produce a certain type of reaction. Frederick's writings, and even to a greater degree Warnery's, are more multi-dimensional then their predecessors or even their contemporaries. Not content to simply describe a particular practice, the two writers discuss the reasons underlying it. Warnery in particular turns to his battlefield experience for examples and to show what is likely to occur under real battlefied conditions.

As a result, Warnery's writing is like a kaleidoscope. In addition to the wide array of material, there is an extremely heterologous treatment. A historical sketch is followed by a theoretical analysis of various manoeuvres. In one place Warnery might discuss battlefield experiences and how they impact on tactical systems, in another he might analyse the advantages and disadvantages of the horses used by the cavalry in each army and how these affected their performance. He might then refer to a conversation with Schwerin, Seydlitz or even Frederick about the efficacy of some cavalry technique.

Remarks on Cavalry appears to have had a marked impact on military art and science in the years immediately following its publication. G. H. Koehler, the translator of the present work, served as an aide-de-camp to Lord Heathfield during the 1790s. Recognizing the value of the original French version, Lord Heathfield never failed to praise the work, which he urged others among the British military to read. It was the work's growing reputation as one of the most comprehensive and thorough treatments of cavalry doctrine that lead to the publication of the English translation in 1798 and then a second edition in 1805. Even after the conclusion of the Napoleonic Wars it was still considered valuable and the last French edition appeared in 1828.

Other circumstantial evidence of Warnery's intellectual impact on the European military intelligentsia can be found. After the battle of Neerwinden (18 March 1793), General Dumouriez' Adjutant would report that the Austrians had used a curious form of a cavalry column of attack with telling effect. The main thrust of the charge was performed by Austrian cavalry in a closed-order column. This was supported by additional cavalry in line which was placed immediately behind the closed column. This was essentially the secret Prussian cavalry column of attack used so successfully by Seydlitz at Zornsdorff, Marshal Gesler at Strigau and Leideritz at Kesslesdorf and described in great detail in Chapter VIII of *Remarks on Cavalry*.

Another example is found in Marshal Ney's *Military Studies:*

Instructions for the Troops Composing the Left Corps, originally written at the camp de Montreuil-sur-Mer in 1804. Ney had set up regimental schools at the camp. To address the deficiencies of the 1791 infantry regulations, as well as to counterbalance a frequent over-reliance on columnar methods of movement and attack, the Marshal penned his own tactical studies. These provided a number of pro-cedures, manoeuvres and practices which, though not officially sanc-tioned by the 1791 regulations, had proven to be effective during the crucible of battle. They also included a description of some techniques that had been successfully employed by the Prussian army during the Seven Years' War. In the section entitled 'Examples of the March in Column to outflank . . . Enemy's Line', Ney describes how to use what the Prussians had called the 'march by lines' manoeuvre to turn and then attack the enemy's flank. Although couched in different terminol-ogy, the concepts underlying these manoeuvres are substantially the same as those that had been described by Warnery in Chapter IX, '*Of the Movements in Oblique Line*'.

Obviously, neither the Austrian cavalry's use of a closed column coupled with a supporting line at Neerwinden nor Ney's description of techniques to outflank the enemy incontestably prove that their respective authors had read *Remarks on Cavalry*. After all, by the 1790s some of the Prussian's better kept secrets gradually became known among the more discerning military circles in Austria, France and England. But the appearance of Warnery's work in 1781/82 and its later translation into English at the very least stimulated and elaborated upon information already circulated by word of mouth, and it is highly unlikely that someone as adept and well versed as Marshall Ney was unfamiliar with the Prussian hussar's work.

Unfortunately, Warnery's celebrity would prove to be short lived. With the end of the Napoleonic Wars, the *Remarks on Cavalry* eventually became a forgotten work. No longer thought of as providing useful, practical information, it was cast aside, like so many other works of the period. Until the 1990s, military historians have only cited his *Des Herrn Generalmajor von Warnery Samltliche Schriften* and *Campagnes de Frédéric II, roi de Prusse, de 1756 à 1762*, and even then only sparingly.

The reappearance of this important work, therefore, is a welcome addition to the primary sources that are available to the modern military historical enthusiast. Undoubtedly it will shed much new light on eighteenth-century warfare and alter some of our assumptions about how warfare of the period was conducted. It is also hoped that its appearance will spark interest in Warnery's other military scientific work.

Plate 1

Hussar Officer

OF

CAVALRY IN GENERAL.

C H A P. I.

THE general term of Cavalry, as commonly received, comprifes every defcription of foldiers ferving on horfeback; the different nature of which, both as to troops and horfes, are further diftinguifhed by the denomination of Heavy and Light.

The firft confifts in Cuiraffiers, Carabiniers, Heavy Troopers, without cuiraffes, and in fome countries may be included the Dragoons; in a word, all that are mounted upon large horfes.

The fecond includes the Light Horfe, Huffars, Hulans, as alfo all the oriental cavalry, which lightly mounted, fight almoft always without regular fyftem or method; as Turks, Tartars, Calmouks, Moors, Cofaques, and other troops of the eaftern nations, fcarcely known in

A   Europe,

Europe, which are called irregular troops, and although divided into feparate corps, or Cornettes, are proper only to lay wafte a country, and by their numbers, to overwhelm fome patrole, or fmall detachment, always avoiding to encounter regular troops formed into corps, and above all, never approaching infantry or cannon.

Cuiraffiers differ only from the carabiniers and other heavy cavalry, in being armed with cuiraffes; having befides, like them, ftraight fwords, carbines and piftols, and a crofs cafque or iron callotte upon their hats; they are mounted upon large horfes, and never fight on foot, but in cafes of abfolute neceffity. The Auftrians, the Danes, and fome fquadrons in France, have, or at leaft had a fhort time paft, cuiraffes before and behind. The Englifh have done wifely to abandon the cuiraffe entirely, and the Auftrians have likewife quitted the one behind, and no doubt but all will follow in this, the example of the Englifh cavalry. The cuiraffiers of other nations have the plaftron only: the braffards, cuiffards, gantletts de lames and bottes ferrés, are entirely laid afide. The Auftrians have yet in Hungary, complete armour for the head.

Dragoons, conformable to their inftitution, ought to be infantry mounted upon horfes, that they might arrive with more expedition to the pofition on which they are to fight on foot; and in a battle they ought to form in line, and act with the infantry. Such was formerly the actual fervice of dragoons, or as they were then denominated, Arquebuffiers on horfeback.

It

Plate 4.

Curassier

Plate 3.

Heavy Dragoon

Plate 15.

It is said to have been the famous Count of Mansfield who baptized them by their prefent name, without doubt upon comparifon with thofe imaginary dragons which are reprefented as fpitting fire.

About the middle of the laft century the Swedes began to make ufe of them as light horfe, to oppofe the Croats of the Emperor, and at the beginning of this, they were mounted upon large horfes, which have fince been exchanged, after the example of the Saxons, for Polifh horfes, as light, ftrong, and excellent for all the operations of war.

The dragoons have preferved the bayonet, and the fame arms as the infantry; the Englifh and Hanoverians only, have the fame as the heavy cavalry, and alfo trumpeters, in which they are right : for how can a drummer do his duty or defend himfelf on horfeback. Dragoons ought to be exercifed on foot, almoft as well as infantry.

There was formerly in European armies, a fpecies of cavalry called lancers: they were armed at all points ; in France they were called Gen's d'Armes, they were all noble or lived nobly, but they could not be employed on all occafions, they were too expenfive, each of them was obliged to have two horfes for his own perfon, a large one for battles and tournaments, and another for marches and detachments ; and befides thefe, one for the fervant who had the care of them : and it was in confequence of the great expence that thefe troops were difcontinued, when the armies were augmented. It is neverthelefs certain, that the lance will always be the Queen of Arms for the defenfive of this nature of cavalry.

A 2

Formerly

Formerly cavalry was eſtimated by lances, and at one time a lance made ten horſes, but this varied at different times.

The French dragoons have caſques or helmets, reſembling the ancient Romans, with a horſe hair creſt inſtead of a feather, formerly they had caps, ſimilar to thoſe of the grenadiers, which was intended to give them a martial air : but I am of opinion that nothing has a better or more military appearance for a ſoldier, than a hat. Caps, or helmets, &c. of whatever form, ſuiting certain faces only.

Before the end of the laſt century, Huſſars were little known, except in Hungary, from whence they derive their origin, they then had clothes almoſt as ample as the Poliſh horſe, and were armed like their Huſſars. It is not an hundred years ſince they quitted the Pique and the Banderolle.

Hungarian Huſſars was a National Militia attached to certain ſtrong places, from whence they made perpetual incurſions againſt the Turks, even in time of peace; by degrees, as the Emperor made conqueſts in Hungary, and had no farther occaſion for all thoſe fortreſſes, moſt of them were raſed or fell into decay of themſelves ; from that time this cavalry was no longer neceſſary, and they were formed into regiments, which were employed in Germany, the Croats were ſent home to guard their own country, and to re-people it : the Turks having almoſt rendered it a deſert, by their frequent incurſions for nearly a century.

The

Plate 7

Plate 8.

Plate 9

Bavarian Light Dragoon

The Croats were precisely what the Huffars are now, and rendered the fame fervice in the armies; they were generally commanded by Italians, or officers natives of Italy, which is the reafon there are found among them, as it is pretended, many families originally from that country.

The advantage of having Huffars with an army, being generally allowed, each Sovereign was defirous of having fome fquadrons of them in his fervice; at firft none were admitted but Hungarians, deferters, or others, but afterwards, Germans were received, and in courfe of time, Poles; and when thofe corps were fucceffively augmented, no preference was given to Hungarians, experience having proved, that it was not neceffary to be born in Hungary to become a good Huffar. I am of opinion, however, that light dragoons would render the fame fervice, in effect to what purpofe to mafquerade the natives of a country, by giving them a Foreign drefs that is more expenfive, and at the fame time, the moft inconvenient that can be imagined? The Auftrian dragoons of Loewenftein, although newly raifed, ferved equally well with the beft Huffars; whofe arms are, a large fabre, very much curved, a carbine and piftols: Polifh, Tartar, and Moldavian horfes, anfwer better for them than Hungarian, thofe being extremely degenerated within thefe fifty years; without doubt, for want of attention to procure ftallions from Turkey, which are found to be the beft in the Hungarian Haras (or ftuds,) and they never had any other, while the Turks were in poffeffion of that country.

It is in the Huffars that the beft officers of cavalry are formed, for this plain reafon, that they are moft frequently in prefence of, and engaged with the enemy, often on detachments, charged with the execution of difficult and delicate enterprizes, affording them frequent

C

oppor-

opportunities of exercifing their capacities, and which obliges them to form their refolutions on the fpot, and determine, without hefitation ; the moft important of all military qualifications.

The Pruffian Generals, Seydlitz, Ziethen, Loffon, and feveral others of diftinguifhed capacity, were taken from that corps. It might like-wife be obferved, that light infantry forms excellent officers of infantry. The Count Lafcy ferved under that famous partifan, Franquini; General Loudon firft began to make his great capacity appear, by ferving amongft the Croats, and Wunch in a free corps ; Count St. Germain was of the fame opinion upon this article with myfelf. The King of Pruffia was fo fully perfuaded of this, that he took officers from the Huffars, to place them in the heavy cavalry ; and when he perceived that an officer of this had a genius for the other, he placed them there for fome years at leaft.

Ulans are no where to be found, except in Poland, unlefs you affimilate them with the pretended Pruffian Bofniacks ; they have faithfully ferved the Kings of the Houfe of Saxony, and the prefent one has three regiments of them in his fervice; they are well mounted and difciplined, and form an admirable corps of light cavalry : they ought to be all Tartars of Lithuania, brave, faithful, and fteady, and by no means drunkards. There are however amongft them, a few Poles; the Republic has alfo a few corps or pulks, but they are by no means in the fame order that the others are. They have preferved their ancient inftitutions ; the Towarifch or Noble Comrades, have their Podftowy or fervants, who are Poles; the Towarifch are the mafters, and the Podftowy the privates, as formerly in France, the latter perform the ordinary fervice. From this originated the cuftom of

counting

Plate 13.

Hulan

Tartar

Plate 12

Plate 5

counting by masters; a hundred masters or lances, formed a thousand horse; the arms of the masters are, a pike with a banderole, (or small flag) a sabre and pistols; those of the servants the same as the Hussars. In an action the latter form in second line in two ranks, in small squadrons, and the masters attack or charge in single rank, which was the ancient custom amongst all the Gen's d'Armes.

The Turkish Spahis, those who receive pay, as well as the Says and the Timars, although they have their standards, and their officers, are not armed uniformly, nor observe any regular order in fighting; some of them have carbines and pistols, others have bows and arrows, as some of the Asiaticks; many have sagayes or javelines, of divers forts; long and short pikes with banderoles; all have sabres or swords, some of the latter of which, are six feet in length, and are carried hanging at the saddle bow, hammers or pole-axes, such as were formerly used in war to break the armour of the cavaliers when unhorsed; a few of them have defensive armour, which consists in a coat of mail or chemissette, a scull-cap of iron, with oreilards, brassards, and gantletts, such as was formerly the armour of our light horse. The Spahis have likewise bucklers of different forms, of wood and of rushes, covered with leather.

The Cosacks have pikes without banderoles, pistols at their belts, and carbines. The Calmoukes are the remains of the ancient Huns, they very much resemble the Tartars, notwithstanding they are not classed into odas, chambers, or cauldrons, as they are; they are however armed like them, and have no other music than that of their Prince, in which they resemble Cosacks, who perform all their military expeditions with silence. The arms of the Tartars are bows and arrows,

some

fome firelocks, a few piftols, and the fabre; fome Hordes have pikes, with a tuft of hair in the form of a banderole.

The carbiniers ought, agreeable to their inftitution, to be armed with rifle carbines, but in feveral fervices they have been taken from them, becaufe it was found by experience, that on horfeback, they had very little advantage, if any, over others. In France there is a fmall number of carbiniers in each company or troop, who ftill retain them. The Auftrians and Saxons have likewife in each regiment of cuiraffiers, a company of carbiniers, who have rifle carbines; at prefent the Auftrians have formed them into feparate corps. In the Ruffian fervice there are a hundred fquadrons of them, who refemble the cuiraffiers in every refpect, except that they have neither collars nor cuiraffes.

It appeared ufeful to enter into this fhort defcription of the different fpecies of European cavalry, to fhew in what they confift, how armed, on what nature of fervice each fhould be employed, and what nature of arms are proper to be oppofed to them.

Cavalry is divided into fquadrons, as infantry is into battalions; a fquadron is from 100 to 200 horfe; and a battalion from 500 to 1000 men; five fquadrons in the Pruffian fervice forms, and is called a battalion of cavalry, becaufe in effect it forms exactly one when they ferve on foot. In that fervice there are regiments of one battalion, and others of two: that is to fay, of five and of ten fquadrons; regiments not being then of the fame ftrength, and the fquadrons being almoft always fo in every fervice, it would be a great error to judge of the ftrength of an army by the number of regiments of which it was

compofed;

compofed; that is a fault into which many very refpectable authors have fallen, we muft therefore eftimate the ftrength of an army by fquadrons and battalions.

Squadrons are fometimes augmented to 200 horfe, though they at prefent confift of no more than 150; and it is to this number which we muft adhere, as well as to 750 men for a battalion, as being a juft medium. I will explain the reafon why that number ought to be ob-ferved, and the advantages which refult from having them thus ftrong: A fingle regiment of ten fquadrons, is preferable to two regiments of five fquadrons each: in the firft there is more union, uniformity, and efprit de corps; they are accuftomed to the fame word of command, and to act in larger bodies; they have an intereft in fupporting each other, without jealoufy; and what is moft effential, they will always be better formed to great manœuvres than fmaller regiments.

However well two regiments of five fquadrons each may ma-nœuvre feparately, the fuperiority of that of ten would be very perceptable, by uniting the two fmaller regiments, and manœuvring them as a fingle corps in prefence of the fingle regiment of ten fquadrons. Alfo more extenfive manœuvres can be performed with ten fquadrons, than with five. The King of Pruffia was fo con-vinced of this, that he made, in confequence, the following arrange-ments, two months before the reviews; when the foldiers who had been on furlough, (bourloubte) rejoined their corps, the troops were exerci-fed by fquadrons, in their quarters, for the fpace of ten or twelve days, after which, the regiments affembled and cantoned in large villages in the neighbourhood of each other, where each regiment ex-

D

ercifed

ercifed complete for one month: afterwards they changed their quarters, two regiments joined and manœuvred together, and when that could be conveniently done, a regiment of cuiraffiers was joined with one of dragoons, or huffars, to equalize them : They reconoitre, alarm, and attack each other reciprocally, until the time arrived for all the troops to affemble at the encampment, they then worked without interruption for fome days; not in fmall corps, but in great orders of battle of every defcription : attacks, retreats, oblique lines, upon all natures of ground, patroles, convoys, foraging parties, nothing was there omitted of all the operations on actual fervice in the field : It is thus that armies ought to be formed every where, and by thefe means young officers and foldiers would foon acquire the quicknefs, precifion, and other qualities of veterans in the fervice.

The more officers there are in the fquadron the better, but in an action there ought not to be at moft more than three in front, the commanding officer of the fquadron in the centre, and one on each flank, more would prevent the foldiers from fighting, and particularly if the fhock or charge fhould not be given with rapidity; in thefe cafes, their horfes, either becaufe they find themfelves preffed upon before and behind, or becaufe they are ftartled at the fwords and the blows, throw themfelves acrofs the line of the charge, which not only renders it impoffible for the officers to defend themfelves, but alfo prevents feveral foldiers in the ranks from doing their duty againft the enemy: it would therefore be better if the officers were in the front rank.

A fhort time before the laft war the King of Pruffia faw the neceffity of this alteration, and fince that time, much fewer officers have been

loft

loft than when they all fought in front of their fquadrons : there muft be fome on the flanks, becaufe from thence they are better enabled to obferve what paffes in the ranks, keep the foldiers to their duty, and the files clofed, &c. for it is generally the flank files which begin to difband firft, thofe in the centre not having the fame facility to do fo : there muft likewife be an officer in the rear of the fquadron with fome confidential non-commiffioned officers to prevent the foldiers from ftragling in the rear, and quitting the fquadron : the Pruffian reglement directs them to be kept to their duty with the fabre if nothing lefs will do it. Thefe officers have alfo the facility of rendering themfelves inftantly to any part of the fquadron where their prefence might be neceffary, either to fill up an interval, to clofe files which might have been thined, or to form a fmall referve in the rear of any part of the fquadron where they prefs too much; for at the moment of the charge, the commanding officer of the fquadron, and the officers which are before the front rank, can no longer fee what paffes in the fquadron, they have enough to attend to their own perfons, and to the enemy who fixes all their attention : and thofe on the flanks fee thofe in their front only, or at moft the files next to them.

Squadrons have been fixed at 150 troopers, exclufive of the officers and noncommiffioned officers, becaufe if they were ftronger, they would be unwieldy and very difficult to manœuvre with precifion and order, efpecially as the greateft force of cavalry now confifts in its rapidity and vivacity; it requires likewife a great deal more time and trouble to rally a larger fquadron : if it confifted of 750 men as a battalion does, it would be impoffible to do it in prefence of the enemy, and this is the reafon why a line of cavalry without intervals, or in muraille is ob-jectionable and dangerous, if on the contrary the fquadron was weaker,

it

it would not be of fufficient weight or impulfe in the charge, and would oppofe too contracted a front to the enemy: to obferve then a juft proportion, it ought to confift of 150 men, or 50 files, in three ranks. It is againft the Turks only that cavalry ought to form line entire without intervals, and then the infantry fhould be formed with them, and the whole manœuvre together, clofe, compact, and flow.

The arrangement of cavalry has frequently varied. Guftavius Adolphus formed his fquadron in fix ranks. Before Henry IV. of France, the Gens d'Armes fought in one fingle rank, and this cuftom has continued ever fince the wars of Louis the fecond with Charles Duke of Burgundy, furnamed the Hardy, and it ftill continues, or at leaft ought to do fo amongft the Poles, if they would act conformable to the inftitution of their arms: the fervans formed alfo little fquadrons in interline two deep, and thefe laft mentioned, though lightly armed for thofe times, were notwithstanding more heavily fo than our cuiraffiers are now: thofe fervans, or as they were called companions of fuccour, threw themfelves fword in hand upon the enemy, the inftant the Gens d'Arms or lancers had made an opening, this was alfo the method in which the nobles fought; for in thofe times all were obliged to ferve either on foot or on horfeback, this was the ban and the arrear ban.

The combat of cavalry was very fharp and brifk, nothing there mechanical, it was the point of honor which animated them, and a noble lancer would have been afhamed to have quitted his hold until he was unhorfed or broke his lance; as for wounds, being armed from head to foot, it was very rare to receive any, and in fpeaking of the combats of thofe old times, we fay, there was fo many lances broke.

In

In the laſt century there was no eſtabliſhed regulation for the attack of cavalry, ſometimes it was done with the ſword, at other times in diſtant carbine or piſtol firing, without doubt, as caprice of the General or commanding officer dictated.

But the moſt uſual attack of cavalry was thus : when two ſquadrons were in preſence of each other, a few files were detached from the right flank of each, to ſkirmiſh againſt the others in their front, and after having diſcharged their arms, they returned to the left of their ranks, and were ſucceeded by others, and this was the practice amongſt the Pruſſian Huſſars not thirty-five years paſt. This ſkirmiſhing laſted a long time before they had recource to their ſwords ; it is known that at the battle of the Dunes, the Spaniſh cavalry received the French with their muſquetoons, and were of courſe ſoon overſet by them.

Quinci relates that the Prince of Orange become King of England, having approached the French army, which was beſieging either Namur or Mons ; Louis XIV. ordered that his cavalry ſhould fight with their fire-arms, which proves how little he was acquainted with the ſervice of that ſpecies of troops, and that he followed the eſtabliſhed cuſtom of fuſilading at a diſtance, until one or the other gave way.

Charles XII. of Sweden, was the firſt who. forbid his cavalry to make uſe of their fire-arms, above all in a battle ; the French and the Spaniſh imitated him in that ſoon afterwards, but the Germans, and particularly the Auſtrians, did not adopt it till very late, and that to their coſt, the muſquetoons were then very ſhort, the ſame as ſome Pruſſian Huſſars have them at this time ; and I am of opinion they exchanged them without any good reaſon, and that they will return into

E   faſhion

fashion again; they were carried flung to the bandouliere, or cross belt, which was not inconvenient; whereas the long carbines are very much so, the muzzle must be put into a cafe or shoe, or have a swivel to fling them to the saddle, and in an action, being obliged to hook them to the belt, they were very subject to get out of order, and break, besides they cannot be leveled except with both hands, whilst the musquetoon could be managed with one.

Formerly when two squadrons charged sword in hand, the most rapid pace was the trot only, here the largest horses afforded the greatest advantage over small ones; files were pressed together very close, which they were enabled to do, from the circumstances of all the troopers being furnished with strong and stiff boots, which with much reason in several services they begin to resume. The King of Prussia's Guards de Corps have them, as well as the officers of his regiments of cuirassiers; they must not however be too heavy, it is sufficient if their weight should not be so great as to prevent those who wear them from walking with ease.

The charge at the walk or trot, is at this time called the ancient attack of cavalry.

When the King of Prussia ascended the throne, he found his cavalry formed to this manœuvre, his horses and his troopers were colossuses they did not dare venture to walk on a bad pavement, or move on uneven ground. He soon perceived that this was good for nothing but parade, and not for service: and that both smaller men and horses would be more proper for that arm; convinced that the real advantage of a squadron consisted in the impetuosity of the shock, the

order

order in which it is given, and the dexterity in handling their swords. He rejected almost entirely the use of fire-arms on horseback, and followed the system of Charles XII. who one day threatened his drabans to take them entirely away, if ever they took it in their heads to make use of them; this I was assured of by an old General officer, who had served in that corps. On some occasions carbines are absolutely necessary, particularly in a retreat in presence of light cavalry, and in qaurters.

Frederick abolished all fire-arm exercise on horseback, as loading by word of command, &c. It must be confessed that the fire of a squadron, which can be made by one single rank only, does not merit any attention to be paid to it; this observation, experience has confirmed, in more than a hundred instances, and I never saw a squadron fire, that was not defeated by that which charged without firing.

Without any intention to derogate from the merit of the late Field Marshal, Kevenhuller, it might be safely affirmed, that the instructions which he gave to his regiment of dragoons, was almost less than nothing, his broken or independant fire was only fit to frighten sparrows; and it is very certain that the fire of a squadron, at best, only tends to throw it into disorder, for if amongst a hundred horses, three or four only are unquiet or restive, when the carbines are cocked, it is sufficient to throw all the others into confusion, however well broke and exercised they may have been, and from that instant it is extremely difficult for the trooper to present his piece, and impossible for him to take any aim, or fire with precision.

The

The Auſtrians gave carbines to the quarter maſters, and non-commiſſioned officers, which had the diſadvantage of engaging them to fire
like ſimple ſoldiers, rather than to attend to their proper duty. In 1760,
they gave pieces called traboues or blunderbuſſes, with very wide muzzles,
and which were loaded with ten or twelve ſmall piſtol balls, to ſome
of the cuiraſſiers of the front rank, but the Pruſſians never perceived
any effect from them.

Since the lance has been rejected, the ſword is, without contradic-
tion, the queen of arms for the cavalry; and it is upon that alone, that
they ſhould depend in action, until the enemy is diſperſed: it is only
then that they might be allowed to make uſe of their piſtols. Opinions
are very much divided with regard to the advantage or ſuperiority
of the edge or the point of the ſword for cavalry in action; each have
their advocates equally zealous, who produce ſuch inſtances as are in
favour of that they prefer: but after much reflection on this important
ſubject, frequent obſervations of the advantages and diſadvantages of
each, and ſome experience, during many years actual ſervice in the
cavalry, I hope I ſhall be permitted to mention my reaſons for giving a
decided preference to the latter.

The point of the ſword is more advantagous than the edge, becauſe
with it you can reach your enemy at a greater diſtance than with the
other, the ſmalleſt wound with it renders the wounded incapable of
ſerving during the remainder of the action at leaſt; it does not require
ſo much force to give a dangerous wound with a thruſt as with
a cut, and the effect of the latter is much more uncertain, unleſs it
happens to be particularly well placed, which it is hardly poſſible to
do, unleſs you have your enemy as it were under your hand: In
ſhort,

fhort, if he has a helmet or hat, with an iron callotte upon it, with large fides, and firmly fixed to the head by a thong or ftrap, he can hardly be touched with the fabre, except in the arm. Charles XII. was fo confident of the fuperiority of the point over the edge, that he gave all his cavalry very long fwords, and fo narrow, that they could be made no other ufe of than to thruft with the point; thofe of the Pruffians are applicable to the fervice of both edge and point, but they appear to be too heavy. The King of Sardinia had the fwords of his cavalry blunted and rounded at the point, to oblige the troopers to make ufe of the edge only. Between thefe two contradictory authorities, I think we may fafely decide in favour of the Swedes, whofe cavalry has performed fuch brilliant actions, whilft that of the Piedmontefe, though well compofed, have never very much diftinguifhed themfelves, either becaufe they have not been fufficiently numerous, or becaufe that the interfected nature of the country in which they ferved, did not permit them : befides, I am informed, they ftill continue to manœuvre in the ancient manner.

Speaking one day with his Majefty the King of Pruffia, of this diverfity of opinions, with regard to the edge or the point, he anfwered, " Kill your enemy with the one or the other, I will never bring you to an account with which you did it."

Experience has fhewn, that forming cavalry fix deep rendered one half of them ufelefs, and that befides the impoffibility of rallying them when thrown into diforder; the deftruction made by artillery in fuch a mafs was enormous. This led to the oppofite extreme of forming in two ranks, but this is equally objectionable, and fhould only be done in cafe of abfolute neceffity; for the prefervation of the foldiers is not

F   the

the principle object to be attended to in the field, but the more important one of defeating the enemy. Ranks fhould therefore be formed two deep only in prefence of an enemy, which we may venture to difpife ; or on fome particular occafions, when it is neceffary to prefent an extenfive front, or in the difagreeable occafion of having too fmall a number of cavalry in the field, and the fquadrons being weak ; this was what the King of Pruffia was obliged to do, much againft his wifh, in the war of 1756.

On the day of the battle Reichenberg, in Bohemia, General Macquire having paffed the Neiffe, below Kratzau, coming from Gabel, had cut us of from our waggons, which were marching from Zittau; he was in the rear of our army with 7000 men. At the moment we began to move forward to the attack, the author of thefe remarks then placed 600 Huffars and Dragoons, which were under his command, in a rank entire, by which General Macquire was deceived; he believed the others to be fuperior in numbers, and retired without attempting any thing. The Duke of Bevern condefcended to acknowledge in a letter, written with his own hand, that to this manœuvre he was principally obliged for the fuccefs of that encounter.

A fquadron ought certainly, except in the particular inftances above-mentioned, to be formed in three ranks, the beft regulated armies have adopted that order, a greater depth would be liable to the objections before mentioned, and a fmaller number of ranks would not have fufficient ftrength nor weight, and would not be enabled to furnifh the fhock in charging: whereas in three deep the two rear ranks not only prefs the firft forward, but prevent them from . ftopping, and any of the troopers from retiring : the horfes themfelves are eager to pufh forwards

when

when they find thofe in the rear ranks preffing upon them, and reaching upon them with their fore feet.

A fquadron formed in two ranks is very fubject to waving, and much eafier broken than one of three, which alfo muft naturally have a greater weight in the fhock, and be much more difficult for an enemy to penetrate, even fhould feveral of the front rank be fallen or difabled: for as it caufes no opening in the line, the horfe will not fail to advance even without his rider, feeling himfelf preffed on each fide and behind, as it always happens: for a horfe muft be very much wounded to make him fall upon the fpot. One without his rider, at Strigau, which had one of his hind feet carried away by a cannon ball, joined the left of the fquadron, where he ran with the others during all the battle, although we were feveral times difperfed; at the found of the call he always fell into the fame place, which was, without doubt, the fame that he had before belonged to in the fquadron.

Another time a curiaffier's horfe fell, in the grand attack at the ex-ercife of Breflau, the cuiraffier got him up again, and mounted him; at three hundred paces he fell down dead. The late General Krokou, Colonel of the regiment, had him opened, and it was found that the fword of the curiaffier had penetrated his heart a tenth of an inch. Thefe facts prove that a horfe is not eafily to be brought fuddenly down, unlefs a ball fhould break his fcull.

A fquadron of 40 or 50 files, in three ranks, is told off into four divifions (in general called Zuge,) and one of 34 and under, into 3; on a march, and on the parade, the officers fall in, in front of their divifions, but in manœuvring they remain upon the flanks, without

however

however being fixed to the one or the other, but are to move to that towards which the divifions are to form into line, or the proper pivot flank, that they may preferve the diftances and intervals, and drefs the line correctly, fo that at the words, *halt front*, or *wheel into line*, the whole may be correctly formed in an inftant, in its proper order, without requiring any alteration; that every one might, without moving, be in their proper place, which could not be fo if the officers who led the divifion remained in the columns, or in the line, where they could only attend to thofe who marched immediately in front.

For inftance, if the line has marched off the ground in columns by the right, the officer fhould march on the left flank of his divifion: and *vice verfa*, fhould the column have marched off by the left. In this manner, without changing their place, or paffing amongft the ranks or divifions in the column, they find themfelves in their proper places as foon as the divifions wheel up and re-form the line.

General officers fhould place themfelves in fuch fituations as to be enabled to fee, if poffible, all the movements and operations of the troops under their command; every other officer fhould, at all times, remain at his poft, whether on a march, at exercife, or in prefence of the enemy; that they may be in readinefs to correct any error in their movements, or in fhort, to give fuch orders as circumftances might require.

The commanding officer of a fquadron being to direct it to the charge, he is in fome fort refponfible for its doing its duty in prefence of the enemy; he fhould therefore not allow any perfon to interrupt or em-

barras

barras him, but to referve his attention free and difengaged from every thing but the movements of the enemy, and the operations of his own fquadron, as connected with the line or wing to which it belongs: He ought to move along the front of his fquadron, from flank to flank, until the trumpeters found the charge. He muft then take his poft, which is in front of the centre of the troop or fquadron: From the moment that the line or wing begins to move forwards, it is no longer time to correct any thing in the ranks or files of the fquadron, which is the reafon that more good-will is required in the cavalry than in the infantry.

What has already been obferved with refpect to the pofition of officers advancing to the charge in front of their fquadrons, is equally applicable to the fault which is committed in thofe armies where the General officers and ftaff, are accuftomed to charge in in the fame manner, their deftruction is almoft inevitable, at the fame time that it renders them incapable of attending to the more important duties attached to their charge, and reduces them to the fituation of private troopers, who would acquit themfelves much better in the manuel exercife of their fabre than an old and perhaps infirm General, whofe lofs however might difcourage the troops, and caufe them to remain inactive during the reft of the combat.

Thefe facts appear to be fufficiently important and convincing, to prevent any more than one field officer being placed in front of a regiment to lead it to the charge; the others, as well as the Generals, ought to remain in the intervals; and perhaps they would be better enabled to obferve and correct any error in the move-

G

ments of the line by being a little in the rear of it. Such is really the duty of their place, and not to be fabring in the front like private troopers. What fhould we think of Generals, or fuperior officers of infantry, who would take firelocks and place themfelves in the front rank, to make ufe of them againft the enemy during an aftion; and yet this is precifely the fame thing.

CHAP. II.

Of the Formation or Composition of Cavalry.

AN army might be confidered as a machine, which is moved at will, and for the conftruftion of which, it is not only neceffary to have good materials, but to know how to form and put them in motion.

Let us premife, that in all countries, where the military are not diftinguifhed, they never will or can have good troops: It was from the fmall eftimation in which they were held under the laft King of Spain, of the Houfe of Auftria, that the armies of that monarchy formerly fo much admired, fell into fuch contempt. Thofe of Portugal had the fame fate under the laft King; thofe of Saxony, under Auguftus III. and thofe of Denmark, under the grandfather of

the

the prefent King; thofe of Poland, by the negleét with which they have been treated fince the time of Jean Sobiefky.

The fpirit and difcipline of an army is foon deftroyed by contempt, but it is a work of time and great exertion to reftore. If the military is not diftinguifhed, what motives can engage perfons of fortune and merit to enter into the fervice?

None but thofe whom mifery purfue, would be in the right to engage in fuch a profeffion.

It is honour alone which can prevail upon perfons in eafy circumftances to embrace a fatiguing and painful way of living, with very little pecuniary advantage, full of dangers, and which in fome fort deprives them of liberty; for fubordination muft there be obferved rigoroufly, without regard to birth or proteétion; I would have a ftriét and fevere difcipline, but not flavery, which vilifies elevated fentiments. That principle is a bad one which would, without attention, animate men by the lafh or the cane like horfes. A foldier, and above all, an officer, muft love his profeffion; but it is not the way to engage him to it by continual calling, and finding fault oftentimes without reafon, as fome commanding officers are fond of doing. The military may be rendered refpeétable, without relaxing in difcipline, fubordination, and refpeét.

For faults which are not criminal, they fhould not infliét chaftifements which fullies his honour and his charaéter: fuch as that of putting officers in irons to make them march at the cannon, even before the crime is enquired into.

Military

Military rank and titles fhould not be beftowed on improper perfons, who ought rather to aim at diftinguifhing themfelves by other means.

It fhould alfo be recollected, that every thing encreafes in price, and confequently that the appointments and allowance of officers, who are obliged to incur greater expences than formerly, fhould not be diminifhed : that Captains at leaft fhould be in a fituation to live commodioufly, becaufe a fubaltern ought to look upon a company as a fortune to which he afpires, and for the acquifion of which, he muft paft through many years of fatigue and dangers, apply all his atten-tion, and exert all his faculties, in many trying and delicate fituations, particularly in a fervice where military diftinctions are not to be pur-chafed or difpofed of, like a mercantile commodity.

In the cavalry none muft be engaged but young men of approved fidelity : and vagabonds or deferters never received, when it is poffible to avoid it; in feveral fervices many regiments of cavaly fail in not attending to this advice.

Huffars, and all thofe who ferve in the light horfe, of every defcrip-tion, ought to be perfons upon whom you can confide and depend : for befides that, at every moment they have it in their power to defert with horfe, arm, and baggage; it is often on their vigilance and fidelity which depends the fafety of a quarter, and even of the whole army.

All nations have not the fame facility of raifing the requifite variety of cavalry equally excellent.

The

Plate 10

Plate 2

British Light Dragoon

British Heavy Dragoon

Plate 21.

Plate 22

Royal Horse Guard

The Spaniards and the Neapolitans have very good horfes for actual fervice during an action: but they are faid to be degenerating very faft, being all ftone-horfes, and fiery, they cannot fupport thofe long marches and fatiguing duties, which are unavoidable in the courfe of a campaign, and particularly in winter: neither the men nor the horfes of thefe nations are proper for our climates.

The Englifh have every thing which can be defired to form an excellent body of cavalry of every fpecies; their light dragoons ought, and does, furpafs every thing which we have ever feen of that nature; and as their cavalry is not numerous, they have the greater facility, in being felect in their compofition, both in men and horfes, without being obliged to have recourfe to other countries, or to look out of their own ifland; an advantage which few countries poffefs.

The French cavalry has been very much neglected, in time of peace a part of them is difmounted, which is not the method to improve them. In France, as every where elfe, the provinces which abound in fields and meadows, furnifh the beft materials for cavalry, whereas in a country of vineyards and manufactories, the peafant hardly knows what a horfe is, therefore each of them ought to be appropriated to that fervice which is moft natural to them; and foldiers for the cavalry chofen from a grafs country, becaufe the men and horfes, which both grow there, are brought up as it were together; it was for this reafon that the Auftrians were always defirous of procuring Silefians for troopers.

The French muft always continue to procure a confiderable proportion of the horfes for their cavalry from foreign nations, as they do at

H

this

this time at a very great expence, unlefs they take to breeding more in their own country than they have hitherto done. It will always be very difficult for them to maintain many Huffars and light dragoons, becaufe being too far from the countries, from whence they procure the horfes proper for that fpecies of troops, they cannot re-mount them without great difficulty and expence.

In thofe fervices, where the captains furnifh the horfes for their own troops, the trooper is a better groom than foldier; no cavalry of that defcription will ever be properly dreffed to grand manœuvres, which as it ruins many horfes, the captain to whom they belong, is interefted in fparing them as much as he can; befides their appointments are not in any fervice adequate to fuch heavy expences as they would by that means be obliged to incur.

The Houfe of Auftria, as well as the other Princes of Germany, France, and Sardinia, procure horfes for their curiaffiers, and other heavy cavalry, from Lower Saxony, particularly Holftien, and from Friezeland, which are not the moft approved: but where are better to be procured? Auftria has, in her vaft eftates of Germany, enough large and ftrong horfes, but they are more proper for draught than the faddle; it would be eafy to remedy that by procuring ftallions from other countries, after having made experiments which would moft improve the race of horfes intended to be bred. The Swifs afford an example of this kind, before the laft war in Italy their horfes were the worft in Europe: but when the Spanifh army marched into Savoy, a great many Dragoons and other troopers, who are in general mounted upon ftone horfes, having deferted to them, the Swifs purchafed their horfes, and I am affured that they have at this time a breed of horfes,

very

very proper for the fervice of cavalry, but it is very certain that they will again degenerate unlefs they continue to fupply their ftuds from the fame, or other foreign countries.

Notwithftanding that the ftates of the King of Pruffia furnifhes pretty good horfes, that Monarch does not make ufe of any of them in his army, he purchafes thofe for his curiaffiers in Holftien, and thofe for the Huffars and Dragoons, are procured from the Ukraine; within thefe few years arrangements have been made to breed horfes in Silefia, proper for the cuiraffiers, but I very much doubt their fuccefs.

The Danes and the Hanoverians have the fineft horfes of the north, and they are very high priced, but as the troop horfes are the property of the captains, there cavalry is not fuperior to thofe who are not fo well mounted, for the reafons before fuggefted. The Swedes and the Norwegeins, have nothing but nags: The Ruffians, by eftablifhing good harras, or ftuds, have fucceeded to breed a fufficient number horfes very proper for their cuiraffiers, and carbiniers; they are not fine, but are ftrong and more durable than thofe of Holftien, from whence they ftill continue to procure fome; in doing which, General Seidlitz was of opinion they were wrong: horfes proper for mounting Dragoons, Huffars, and other light cavalry, being abundant in their own meridional provinces.

Marfhal Schwerin told me that when the King of Pruffia augmented his Huffars, by the numerous corps which he raifed in addition to the fix fquadrons only, which he had when he came to the throne, he had propofed to the King to form regiments of Light Dragoons, and

in

in my opinion he was not in the wrong, agreeable to the trivial proverb, "It is not the drefs that makes the man."

For a foldier to be really a light horfeman, he muft be able to turn his horfe quick and fhort, when in full fpeed, to raife up and catch any thing from the ground; he will find himfelf much firmer in his feat, have greater command of his horfe, and much more agility in the ex- ercife of his arms, &c. by being mounted on an eaftern faddle, that is to fay, upon a Hungarian, Turkifh, or Polifh one; to thofe who have been accuftomed to other faddles, they appear at firft to be inconve- nient, but they very foon find themfelves perfectly at eafe in them, and ever after, prefer them to all others; they are very light, cheap, and durable, and do not fo often require repairing as the others do. *(See the plate.)*

The fervice of light horfe requiring them to be as it were always in prefence of the enemy, and ready to mount on horfeback in an inftant; they ought not to have either breaft-belts or cruppers to their faddles, which will enable them to faddle much quicker than they can do otherwife: befides, as the faddles above defcribed have double girths, they are fufficiently firm without them.

A light horfeman ought to be careful not to overburthen his horfe, as the Saxons are accuftomed to do; a fhirt or two, and a few other fmall neceffary articles; a nofe bag to give oats to his horfe, in which the implements for dreffing him are put, is all that fhould be allowed; in fact, to what ufeful purpofe are all thofe ample Hungarian holfters; thofe enormous broad crofs belts, echarpes, and fabletaches, and thofe other ornaments of the Huffars, loaded with buttons, plates, cords,

and

Plate 19

Moorish Horse

and taffels, unlefs to create expence to the Sovereign, and incommode the man and the horfe? except in the King's horfe guards, every appointment of the cavalry fhould be plain: befides that, thefe ornaments of lace, &c. coft a confiderable fum of money, which might be applied to more ufeful purpofes : they are foon worn out, and refemble fringes of rags, and look pityful; nothing is more proper and foldier-like for a trooper, than a fimple, plain, and neat equipage, which it is not pof-fible to have for any length of time, whilft covered with all this frippery, more proper for the drefs of a lackey, than that of a foldier.

A good goat or fheep's fkin, fhould be ufed inftead of a houffe, they will cover at the fame time, the piftols and the portmanteau; the bridle alfo ought to be as light as poffible, without any unneceffary buckles or ftraps; there fhould be but one attached to the pommel of the faddle, to ftrap on the cloak rolled up before the trooper, which will be very important, to protect his belly from a thruft with the bayonet or fword, the ftirrups fhould be bronzed; and by thefe means, the trooper, on his arrival at camp or quarters, has but few ftraps and buckles to clean. He covers his arms, accoutrements, &c. with the goat-fkin, and has time to attend to his horfe and himfelf; in fhort, every thing fhould be light and proper, without affectation. I have been informed, that except as to the faddles, the Englifh regiments of Eliott, and Burgoyne, are thus equipped.

The Huffars do not require tents, and the Dragoons might do equally well without them, no light troops are better appointed or more active or allert on horfeback, than the Polifh Ulans: the equi-page and appointments of the Ulan and his horfe, are admirable, com-modious and proper: and although I am not very partial to thofe of

I
the

the Hungarians, yet I am perfuaded it is very proper for feveral nations, particularly thofe in which it is the national drefs.

In every fpecies of cavalry the man ought to be proportioned to the fize of his horfe, and the arms with which he is to ferve, adapted and proportioned to them both, and the nature of fervice to be performed; confequently the cuiraffier fhould be larger, and his arms heavier than the dragoon, and thofe more fo than the Light Horfe or Huffars; a fmall man has great difficulty to mount a large horfe, particularly with a cuiraffe, they fhould all however be mufcular and robuft, but not heavy; the Pruffian Dragoons are too heavy for their horfes, and it is ridiculous to fee a large man upon a fmall horfe: which by being ftrained with too much weight, is very foon ruined, and the trooper difmounted; a man who is more than 5 feet 8 inches, ought not to be received into the cavalry, but will find his proper place in the infantry.

When a recruit is enlifted he is taught to hold himfelf upright, to march with an eafy air, and to fhake off the lounge of the peafant; he is taught the exercife of the broad-fword, with fmall bafket-hilted fticks; nothing contributes more towards rendering him active and dexterous; he is exercifed on foot, until he is fufficiently prepared to begin it in the fquadron. Whatever may be faid, I hold it very ef-fential, that cavalry foldiers, and particularly dragoons, fhould be ac-quainted with the exercife on foot, almoft as well as the infantry; but always in two ranks, as the cuiraffiers; they may alfo preferve their bayonets, provided they are not too weighty: the Englifh and Hano-verians have taken them from their cavalry. It is however very ad-vantageous that cavalry fhould be enabled to defend themfelves at all times, and even on foot, if neceffity required it, and it might be proved

that

Plate 20.

Hulan Trotting

that fuch occafions have, at all times, in every fervice, occured with every nature of cavalry.

It will be found very ufeful to practice on foot, at leaft once, any manœuvres which you would perform with the fquadron, before you try them on horfeback, this not only faves the horfes, but very much affifts the ready and correct conception and execution of it, particularly fhould it be an intricate or complex manœuvre.

When the recruit is fufficiently inftructed on foot, he is mounted upon a wooden horfe, much like thofe made ufe of in riding-fchools for vaulting, but it muft have a neck and head, to fix a bridle to; there fhould be two of thofe horfes per troop, the recruits muft be inftructed by them how to place the faddle on their horfes, to mount and difmount on both fides, with or without ftirrups, how to fold his cloak, to put on his baggage, and a trufs of forrage, to vault into the faddle without aid by the croup, that he might be enabled to do it on his horfe, without having occafion for a knot inftead of a ftirrup; he muft be exercifed to bend forward and take his hat from the ground; to difmount, to ftand and hold the bridle properly; in a word, every thing but vaulting; to place himfelf in every pofition of the exercife, to draw, handle, and return his fword; to load and fire his carbine and piftols; and to exercife and make ufe of his arms with fpirit and addrefs: this is the manner in which recruits are formed in the fervice, and is very nearly the fame that is recommended by Vegecius.

Thefe two wooden horfes fhould be placed as in a rencounter, on the right hand of each other, and thofe that are upon them fhould thruft and cut with the point and with the edge, with

bafket-

bafket-hilted fticks, and they fhould be taught all the guards, to ward off, and to parry the fame.

A foldier fhould not be taught to ride as it is practifed by profeffed riding-mafters, becaufe the greateft part of the aids given by them muft be with the bridle, which for that purpofe muft be held fhort, but without ftiffnefs, the left fhoulder a little forward, extending his hand in an eafy manner to the mane of the horfe; a trooper in the ranks can give falfe aids only with his legs. When he has been properly exercifed in this manner, his horfe is given to him, and he is quartered with a non-commiffioned officer, or fome old fteady trooper, who is to fhew him how to take care of his horfe, how to faddle and to bridle it, to comb his mane without tearing out the hair, and never to touch the tail but with his hand, to wafh it once a week, and after the new moon to cut the points of the hair; experience has proved this to be the true means of preferving that fine ornament of a horfe.

He is alfo to be fhewn how to take care of his arms and accoutrements, faddle and bridle, &c.

The officers fhould affift in teaching him to ride; the riding-mafter cannot attend to all the recruits: befides, he is in general fully oc-cupied in breaking horfes, &c. for the officers.

Every thing fhould now be taught the recruit which might be re-quifite on actual fervice, very near the exercife of the caroufel, except the exercife of the javelin, which would be ufelefs to him. He ought to be able to turn his horfe fuddenly upon his haunches, to run at

the

the ring with his fword inftead of a lance, which very much fuples the
horfe, and forms the trooper to dexterity and firmnefs in his feat, without however attending to all the minutia required in the riding-
academies.

Each garrifon fhould have a covered riding-houfe to exercife in
during the winter, but it is of courfe impracticable where the troops
are difperfed about in villages, which is certainly very prejudicial to
them.

A fquadron ought to be often exercifed without faddles, and manœuvre every day at leaft half an hour: this is abfolutely neceffary,
to keep the horfes in wind, and to harden them; it is with them as
with racers, if they are not kept in continual training, they are very
foon incapable of performing the fervice required of them.

There are few horfes but which might be made to run; when we
had bought thofe which our Huffars had taken from the enemy, the
greateft number of them were given in the re-mount; at firft thofe
troopers who receieved them where difatisfied with their want of activity,
but after having felt the Pruffian fpur for a few weeks, they were as
fleet as the others.

As foon as the fquadron is mounted the troopers are practifed to leap
ditches, enclofures, poles put acrofs for that purpofe, &c. at other times
two troopers run together full fpeed, trying to get before and carry
off each others hats; they are practifed to fwim their horfes acrofs
rivers; to manœuvre in broken and interfected ground; to climb and
defcend heights; they attack in fingle ranks, crofs hollow ways, villages,

K

defilés; in breaking off upon the divifion oppofite to it, they form up rapidly, difperfe, rally, &c. at other times they practife the pofting of grand guards, and vedettes; they reconnoitre, fcour the woods, retreat fighting, difmount and re-mount, deploy, and they muft be made to trot a good deal, by which they will acquire a firm feat on horfeback, and not to fall upon the faddle at each motion of the horfe; they ought to ride with fhorter ftirrups than in the riding-fchools, beacaufe they muft be able to raife themfelves four inches above the faddle.

There are targets to be fired at by the troopers, with their piftols, walking, trotting, and full gallop, and even in leaping over a bar.

When the fquadron arrives at a ditch, the commanding officer gives the word *ditch;* (in German, *graben*) the two rear ranks, if they are in three, inftantly halt, and the firft fprings forward and leaps it, calling out *leap*, and fucceffively the centre and rear ranks, the horfes, by accuftomed to the found of that word, very rarely fail when they hear it.

A head of felt, ftuffed with wool or ftraw, is fixed to a branch or poft, which the foldier is to touch with the thruft or the cut, both in paffing and repaffing, in full gallop. It would very much ftimulate the foldiers to emulation, by attaching fome gratification to thofe who acquit themfelves with the greateft addrefs.

They fhould frequently be made to move brifkly forward, and then fuddenly halted upon the fpot; at the word *halt*, the trooper preffes upon his ftirrups, keeping his body a little backward, retaining the bridle by bending his wrift a little, but without moving his arm; by thefe means he puts his horfe upon his haunches.

A

A fquadron fhould be accuftomed to move off its ground at once, and all the troopers to be in motion at the fame inftant, at the word of command, either at a walk, trot, or gallop ; they fhould even be made to traverfe in line. It will fometimes happen that when they are not perfect in this exercife, fome horfes will receive atteintes, or blows with their fore feet, from the others, but the performance of this manœuvre on fervice, is too important to prevent their acquiring it under any apprehenfions of this inconvenience. It is abfolutely neceffary that good cavalry fhould be able to traverfe, and that they fhould move the whole line at the fame inftant, and not fucceffively, as I have feen it practifed by fome which has rather the appearance of counter than traverfe marching ; nothing can contribute more towards fupleing of horfes than the traverfe movement. It is pityful to fee a fquadron be obliged to break off by divifions to gain ground obliquely to the right or the left, when by traverfing this is performed in an inftant, and gracefully.

A fquadron ought often to be exercifed in a fingle rank, and to advance obliquely to the right and left, upon a variety of alignements and points of view, and appui, in a rank entire ; the faults are more eafily difcovered, and the trooper learns to march in line with more exactnefs : for which purpofe more attention and accuracy is required, an extenfive line in fingle rank being much more fubject to waving than in two or three ; fometimes even the whole regiment fhould manœuvre in this manner.

Seidiltz communicated to me a project which he had conceived fome years paft, and which would then have been put into execution, but

for

for the envious jealoufy of fome perfons who by their intrigues tra-
verfed and prevented it; he had within his own infpeƈtion (and diftriƈt)
in Silefia; about an hundred young gentlemen belonging to the regiments under his command, who are denominated in the cavalry, (ftandards junkers) or gentlemen ftandard bearers; they are all noble (*i. e.*
gentlemen) but have the rank, the pay, and the uniform of non-commiffioned officers; in the infantry the two eldeft wear the fword-knot the
fame as the officers. He had intended to have affembled them at Ohlau,
his head quarters, and to have exercifed, manœuvred, and formed them
to the military evolutions himfelf; they were to have been likewife in-
ftruƈted in foreign languages, the mathematics, &c. and all the bodily
exercifes which form the accomplifhments of a well-bred young gentleman, intended for the army.

On the affembling of the regiments, two months before the reviews,
each of them were to rejoin the regiments to which they belonged, in
order to exercife with them. It is very certain thefe young gentlemen
acquire no fort of ufeful knowledge in the fmall garrifons to which they
are ufually attached in the provinces; but on the contrary, their morals
are in great danger, at that early period of life, of being corrupted,
by paffing too much of their time in taverns, or coffee-houfes, or in low
company; whereas with Seidlitz, they might have made a great progrefs in every fcience and exercife, proper to form a gentlemen and a
foldier, and the whole expence to the King would not have
exceeded fifty ducats per month, for the falary of the teachers, &c.
this arrangement, had it taken place, could not have failed to have been
very advantageous, and would be equally fo in every fervice, where
it is defired to have a good corps of cavalry.

Some-

Something of this kind was likewife propofed at Varfovie, but which from fimilar obftacles, had the fame fate: for it is difficult to render a Polifh noble or gentleman, fufceptible of difcipline in his own country; abroad he is excellent and admirable: but in Poland, that fpirit of liberty, or rather licentioufnefs which pervades every thought and action, prevents him from fubmitting to the fmalleft inconvenience.

C H A P. III.

Of Intervals.

MUCH has been faid on both fides for and againft intervals, but nothing feems hitherto to have been decided to the fatisfaction of all parties ; it would be prefumption to fuppofe that any thing which can be here adduced, will have better fuccefs: but yet it might be ufeful to exhibit the reafons which feems to make it rational and advantageous to adopt the practice of allowing intervals between fquadrons, and to explode the pernicious cuftom of manœuvring en muraille.

The idea of cavalry charging en muraille, is not of antient date; the laft war intervals were very properly left between fquadrons; Prince Louis, of Baaden, was the firft who ventured to abolifh them, but only againft the Turks: and in this, however contradictory it might appear, he was alfo right, for it is in fact againft them only that a

L   corps

corps of cavalry ought to be formed en phalanx; becaufe then it is of the utmoft importance, to remain clofe, compact, and firm; advancing with a flow fteady pace, the cavalry incorporated with the infantry, as is explained in the Treatife on the Turkifh military, by the author of thefe remarks.

Puifegur, whofe information with regard to the fervice of cavalry, was very fuperficial, would have it form fimilar to the infantry, en phalanx or without intervals, and propofes that both fhould march together with equal ftep, in line, to the attack of an enemy; he fuppofes that a line without intervals, encountering one which has them equal to the length of their fquadrons, would have a certain advantage, by means of the fquadrons oppofite to the intervals, wheeling to the right and left by wings, (or half fquadrons) and attacking them on each flank, at the fame time that the fquadron in their front attacked them ftraight forward: however plaufible this may appear in theory, a little confideration will difcover its ferious defects: befides, a line with fuch intervals as therein premifed, is almoft as defective as that en murialle, and both ought equally to be rejected.

The King of Pruffia appears at one time to have adopted the maxim of Puifegur, and that perhaps to his difadvantage, for whenever his cavalry has attacked in this manner, it has always been broken and routed by the enemy, and that frequently, even after a fuccefsful charge.

After the battle of Prague, a letter was written to the late General Winterfeld, to be laid before the King, with obfervations relative to this fubject, but what effect it produced has not tranfpired.

A

A line of cavalry en muraille, even at exercife, cannot manœuvre without confufion ; there would be no objection if it was made ufe of only there, for cavalry accuftomed to manœuvre without intervals, will do it with much greater facility and preciffion, and find themfelves very much at at their eafe when they have them : It is however dangerous to accuftom troops to manœuvre differently at exercife from what they are intended to do in prefence of an enemy, as all officers who might have the command of troops under fuch circumftances, are not decided enough to adopt the variations proper to the fervice required. Some of them would not even reflect whether the manœuvres they had been accuftomed to perform, were better than any other or not ; befides, the effect that fuch alterations, at fuch a moment, might have upon the confidence of the troops.

Cavalry ought therefore to manœuvre on all occafions, both at exercife, as well as in prefence of the enemy, with proper intervals.

Firft. Becaufe a horfe cannot turn upon the fame fpace of ground that it occupies in the ranks, as a man can ; the application of this rule will appear hereafter.

Second. A line en muraille rarely arrives to the pofition of the enemy in order, or rather it never does if the charge is brifk and rapid ; the leaft obftacle in the way of any part of the line deranges it, and this diforder is immediately communicated to the whole, of which it forms a part.

It is fcarcely poffible for a line without intervals to advance for any diftance without waving, the leaft accident throws it into diforder, whether the files prefs too much together, or whether they feparate

and

and form intervals, which they fuddenly incline to clofe up again, they equally break the line, fo that frequently a whole fquadron is obliged to fpring forward, or to fall back into the rear to make room; and when the rapid part of the charge is began, it will be impracticable for them to attempt to re-enter. The charge muft be given fuch as it happens to be: and if it fhould be fuccefsful even in the firft fhock, the caufes above-mentioned will operate to throw it into fuch confufion, as to prevent their taking the proper advantage of it; and an enemy who has his fecond line in fquadrons, with intervals under is hand as it were, will very eafily oblige fuch a confufed mafs to abandon their firft advantage.

In fpeaking of the attack, it will appear of what importance it is that a fquadron or line fhould be enabled to rally inftantly after a fuc-cefsful charge, which it is almoft impoffible to do without intervals; one horfe is faced one way, another the other, they wifh to avoid trampling upon thofe who are down, that officer muft be helped up; this diforder is unavoidable, even in a victorious fquadron, after the charge, and muft be re-formed as quick as poffible. How is that prac-ticable without intervals? the horfes length preventing them from turning except by three's or four's, whereas with intervals they can open a little towards the flanks, and in a moment they are re-formed.

If a line of fquadrons with intervals meets with an obftacle, or even feveral of them at the fame time, they can eafily be avoided and paffed, by inclining a little to either flank, or by doubling off from the centre or flanks, without deranging in the leaft the reft of the line, or being obliged to remain in interline.

If

If a line en muraille detaches a few files to harrafs an enemy in retreat, how are they to be fupported or covered while advancing? if driven in, how are they to re-form into the line? and what confufion do they not caufe in doing fo? which might all be avoided and rendered eafy, by feparating the fquadrons.

The line en muraille is a true phalanx, and the phalanx has always been, and muft remain an unweildy machine, very improper for every operation which requires rapidity; this formation therefore deprives cavalry of its moft effential and important advantage, its impulfe and impreffion confifting not lefs in the rapidity of its action than in its mafs and weight.

Puifegur did not recollect that his half fquadrons wheeling by the intervals, upon the flanks of the oppofite fquadrons, would themfelves be expofed to be taken in flank by the enemy's fecond line, which would fubject them to be inevitably defeated, and rifk involving their whole firft line in their retreat; this could not fail to happen from their being attacked in the moment of confufion, produced in that line by the wheeling of fo many half fquadrons: provided they are attacked with brifknefs and fpirit.

Such large intervals as Puifegur propofes, ought not however to be adopted, his fquadrons would be too far from each other; the medium ought to be prefered; from twenty to twenty-five paces, will be fufficient to prevent their being cramped in their movements upon the flanks. It will however frequently happen, that even thefe will be loft before they arrive at the enemy's line; in a charge, a horfe turning a little from the true line of direction, efpecially if it fhould be on the

M

direct-

directing flank, will be enough to make the fquadron incline too much to the right or left, if they have not a diftinct point of view determined.

The effect however of fuch irregularity will not be very prejudicial, where proper intervals are allowed, nor derange the reft of the line, but may be eafily corrected; and even fhould a whole fquadron in fuch a line be repulfed and broken, it would not involve the reft of them in its misfortune, and a fingle fquadron of the fecond line or the referve immediately remedies it; but fhould this accident happen to the phalanx, it could not be fo eafily done.

A firft line without intervals being beaten, is certain to involve the fecond in its misfortune, by the confufion unavoidable amongft fuch a mafs in retreat, even fhould the fecond line be formed with intervals, they will not wait to examine where they are, efpecially fhould the enemy follow up his fuccefs with fpirit and impetuofity.

Thus by forming a firft line en muraille, the advantage of a fecond line is loft, and thofe troops rendered incapable of any thing but in-creafing the confufion and defeat.

Small divifions of about 20 light horfe, placed oppofite to the in-tervals in interline, would effectually protect the wings of the fquadrons of the firft line from any attack of the half fquadrons of the enemy's charge, in the manner propofed by Puifegur: or the fecond line might be placed within a hundred yards of the firft, which would have the fame advantage: for what enemy could be fo rafh as to prefent fo many flanks of half fquadrons to a complete line? or if he fhould commit fo great an error, would he not be quickly punifhed?

An

An idea will be communicated in the following part of thefe remarks, to combine the impulfe of the order en muraille, with that of the line with intervals, without being fubject to the inconveniencies of either, as has been already mentioned in the the fixth volume of the military remarks, by the fame author.

It fhould always be recollected, that as the force and effect of cavalry confifts in the rapidity of its action, combined with the impetus of its fhock, and the order in which it is communicated, every thing that militates againft thefe effential principles, fhould be carefully guarded againft and rejected.

CHAP. IV.

Of the Attack, or Charge.

A Line or wing of cavalry being formed in order, and on the ground from whence it is to move forward to the charge: the officer who has the command of it muft be careful that it is parallel to the enemy's line; having neglected this precaution at the battle of Prague, our whole left wing inclined too much to the left, and formed an interval between us and our infantry, into which, by the time we arrived to the enemy, ten fquadrons of cavalry might have entered in front.

The

The officers commanding fquadrons fhould agree amongft themfelves upon certain points of view, upon which to direct their attacks ; it might otherwife happen for two fquadrons to charge upon the fame point, which would create great confufion ; fhould, for inftance, any rifing ground, bufhes, &c. intercept the view of the enemy's line, or regiments which are to be charged, fome other object obferved to be in the direction of them muft be chofen, and all the officers ought to be informed that the attack of the fquadron is to be directed upon fuch a height, fteeple, bufh, tree, &c. but if the enemy can be diftinctly feen, they are to be fhewn a particular ftandard, as the 8th, 9th, 10th, &c. from the right or left, upon which they are to direct their charge ; every one muft be acquainted with it before they move off their ground, becaufe, if the officer who leads the fquadron fhould be wounded in the time of the charge, the fquadron not being properly conducted, for want of the others being acquainted with the point of attack, might crofs upon another, whereas when that is known to them all, a fquadron will be enabled to continue the attack, notwithftanding fuch accident ; it is likewife almoft impoffible for an officer to place himfelf in front of a fquadron, and take the command of it when they have preffed forward with both fpurs, but the officers upon the flanks being acquainted with the point of attack, will be able to conduct the charge without quitting them.

It is premifed, that the General has taken meafures for the protection of the flanks of his cavalry whilft charging; and if poffible, made fuch a difpofition as to enable it to gain thofe of his enemy, this will be more particularly treated of hereafter.

If

It is not always neceſſary for cavalry to regulate their movements by thoſe of the infantry, it will ſuffice if they are near enough to attract a part of the fire of the enemy's artillery, and to anſwer it; to prevent the whole of that fire from being directed upon the cavalry, in the moment that it is advancing to the charge; it ſhould therefore move forward ſo ſoon as the cannonade has commenced on both ſides, but from that period ſhould not regulate its movements by thoſe of the infantry; whoſe attack will be very much facilitated by the operations of the cavalry, engaging or defeating that of the enemy ; at leaſt at-tracting their whole attention : ſhould they ſucceed in obliging the enemy's cavalry to retire, and leave the flank of their infantry uncovered, or, as it is called, in the air ; the affair is completed by the attack of the infantry, aſſiſted by a few ſquadrons of the reſerve, falling upon that unprotected wing, as it happened towards the concluſion of the battle of Prague, which decided it in our favour.

It was by manœuvring in this manner that Seydlitz gained the moſt complete victory at Roſbach ; and it is by ſuch decided ſtrokes, that cavalry alone will be frequently enabled to determine the ſucceſs of a battle ; for this purpoſe, the moſt prompt and rapid movements are neceſſary, without balancing or heſitating that the enemy's cavalry may be quickly diſpatched, and obliged to abandon the flank of their infantry.

A General officer, on ſuch occaſions, ſhould always have ſeveral orderly officers, or active intelligent Aids de Camp, well mounted, near him, to carry his orders, and a trumpet to give ſignals, to which all others ſhould anſwer, or repeat the ſame ſound ; Seydlitz always had ſeveral well-mounted Huſſars near him, which were very uſeful.

N   The

The wings generally drefs by each other, or upon a point of apui, which however is of little ufe in the operations of cavalry, and totally ufelefs, as foon as the lines have chofen their points of view, and began to move.

At the firft found of the trumpet the whole begin to move forward, firft and fecond line, and the referve: The attacking wing perfectly dreffed in line, marches on at a walk; at the fecond found, which ought to be doubled, the whole begin to trot, (which the fecond line, and the referve, continue to do till after the charge is finifhed) at the third found, which is tripled, at about 150 or 200 paces from the enemy, the firft line begins to gallop, and when they approach within 70 or at moft 80 yards of the enemy, the trumpets found gay and lively fanfares or flourifhes of the trumpet, then the troopers prick with both fpurs, and pufh forward at full fpeed, without however entirely flackening the bridle, as all the horfes cannot gallop with equal velocity; but when within about twenty paces, they muft force their gallop as much as poffible, to give the full impulfe of the charge, or as the King of Pruffia ufed to call it, the grand coup de collier; the rear ranks muft then alfo prefs forward with all their weight and fpeed, as if they would force forward their front ranks or file leaders; this is called furnifhing the fhock.

The troopers of the front rank raife their fwords to the height of their faces, the arm extended in tierce, the point againft the eyes of his enemy, and the hand a little turned, that the branch or guard of the fword may cover his own; they muft raife themfelves a little in the ftirrups, the body forward, and aim to place a thruft with the point againft the man or the horfe oppofed to him; in a word, he muft do his beft,

either

Plate 11

Light Dragoon Charging

Plate 18.

Front Rank Charging

either by thrufting or cutting, to difable his enemy; thus the fhock or charge is foon finifhed.

The charge being fuccefsful, and the enemy's line broken, the word halt muft be given, and the appel, or call, founded; the whole in the mean time continue to advance flowly, which will render it much eafier to rally, than if the fquadron remained upon the fpot: but they muft difpatch, and no time be loft in examining whether each trooper has exactly fallen into his place; the trumpets then re-commence the fanfares, and the line moves forward again full gallop to purfue the enemy, before they have time to recollect themfelves: The fecond line muft then be charged brifkly during the confternation and diforder occafioned by the defeat and confufion of the firft; this line being obliged then to retreat, the appel, or call, muft be again founded, the line reformed, and no time loft in following up the enemy; without however hurrying fo much as to do it in diforder, or prefling forward too much, to prevent putting the horfes out of wind; but when there happens to be a defilé, through which the retreating enemy is obliged to pafs, they muft there be prefled with the utmoft vigour: it is there that the greateft carnage takes place, which it will be perhaps beft to prevent, as the battle is already gained, it will be more humane and honourable to make them prifoners.

Some officers would have a divifion of each wing of the fquadron in the firft line detached to purfue the enemy: but at prefent, when there is with all armies fo many Huffars and Light Horfe, it is better to leave that to them, for which their horfes are properly adapted, they muft however be fupported by regular clofe fquadrons of cavalry.

The

The General feeing it is out of the power of the enemy's cavalry to re-appear, at leaft for fome time, might make a quarter wheel with his cuiraffiers and heavy cavalry, and fall upon the infantry in flank and rear; or a part of the two lines might be employed for that pur-pofe. As foon as the enemy's cavalry is pufhed beyond their infantry, a part of the fquadron of the firft line might be detached to fall in column on the flank of their fecond line of infantry, and other fqua-drons of the fecond line to do the fame to their firft: thofe fquadrons fimply wheel to the right or left, according to the wing they are to attack; this manœuvre muft be executed with quicknefs and rapidity, and the whole continue to move forward at the trot, at the fame time; during the operation, the firft line, if fo commanded, will, when at the proper diftance, charge the enemy in front, whilft the co-lumns are engaged on their flanks, the fecond line continues the trot, and preferves its diftances of 250 or 300 yards in the rear of the firft, and avoid as much as poffible trampling upon thofe of the firft line, which may have been difmounted or difabled by the enemy during the charge. This line fhould be formed with intervals equal to the front of the fquadrons; and the referve fhould have even larger in-tervals than thofe, and would be more properly placed without, or beyond the extremities of the lines, than in the rear of them. The foldiers of the rear ranks fhould be careful to keep the points of their fwords upright that they may not wound their file leaders.

When it is reflected, what bruifes a trooper is liable to in his legs, with the prefent fuple boots, from the holfters, knees, carbines. fcab-bards, &c. of each other, when the fquadron charges clofe and firm as it ought to do, to give it weight and effect. I think it will not be de-nied, that ftiff boots, which will defend the trooper from fuch ac-
cidents,

cidents ought to be given him ; they will at the fame time enable him to charge clofer in line, than they have ever been able to do fince fuple boots has been adopted, will give him greater firmnefs and confidence on horfeback ; and allow him to fix his whole attention upon his enemy, inftead of being obliged to divide it to parry the wounds he might receive from him in front, and the bruifes from the troopers on each fide ; ftrong boot-tops remedy, in a fmall degree, the evil abovementioned but does not entirely remove it ; both thofe and the boots fhould be worn much higher, fuch as the regiment of Seydlitz has began to make ufe of.

It will eafily be conceived what terrible blows muft be given by two brave troopers who meet each other in the charge ; many people are however of opinion, that the fhock of two lines of cavalry never takes place, one always giving way before the other arrives to it ; though this is moft frequently the cafe, it is neverthelefs an error to fay, that always happens ; at the battle of Guaftala the fhock was general : at Strigau likewife, and in which the Saxons loft a number of officers ; at the battle of Sohre, the Pruffians the fame, and on many other occafions. At Reichenberg, General Purpurati received us with his piftols. and after the difcharge, advanced fome paces only, fword in hand ; but there was then a real fhock given, in which he was defeated.

This is called the regular attack of cavalry, when the order of battle is formed in the ufual manner, the cavalry on the wings, and the infantry in the centre, without chicane, or fineffe, the importance and effect of cavalry, in this cafe, depends as much upon the order and preciffion, as upon the rapidity and courage of the charge ; and moft

O   fre-

frequently determines not only its fuccefs, but the fate of the day likewife.

It fhould be fixed in the mind as an invariable and univerfal axiom, that in whatever fituation or pofition a corps of cavalry might happen to be, it fhould never wait for the enemy's charge; for in that cafe its defeat would be certain and unavoidable, all the perfonal bravery and refolution in the world, would not be able to prevent it : but on the contrary, as foon as it is perceived that coming to blows is una-voidable, they fhould immediately, without hefitation, move forward to the charge ; the decided manner in which this is performed, has the greateft effect upon the confidence and firmnefs of both, and is the only certain means to prevent being defeated, and moft likely to infure that of the enemy.

But fince the enormous augmentation of artillery, it is doubtful whether cavalry ought ever to be formed in the order of battle abovementioned, or even in the firft line at all ; and the wings of infantry are at prefent in general too well covered, to admit of their being fo often attacked in flank by cavalry, as was formerly done ; Monf. St. Germain com-plains, that even in his time the heavy cavalry of France no longer ren-dered any fervice, neither on detachments nor in the field.

CHAP.

C H A P. V.

Of Flanks.

THE flanks are the weak parts of an army, or any other body of troops, therefore too many precautions cannot be taken for their fecurity. Infantry have much greater facility in fecuring their flanks than cavalry, becaufe they are equally proper for the defenfive and offenfive, and can therefore, when on the defenfive, decide the fuccefs of an action without moving from their pofition, if attached in it; which enables them to take every advantage of the nature of the ground, to protect both their front and flanks, by works; a hedge, a ditch, a hollow way, and other innumerable accidental irregularities, or variation in the nature of the ground and country, are fo many defences and advantages to them, which would be as many obftacles to the movements of cavalry, who muft not (as before faid) wait upon their own ground for the attack of their enemy; thus no apui or protection for their flanks, or front, can be of much advantage to them, as they cannot, in the firft inftance, adapt their formation to fuch protection, except with great inconvenience and difficulty, and muft entirely abandon it, as foon as they move forward to encounter the enemy; as they muft always do when attacked. Ditches, interfecting hollow ways, &c. would tend only to embarrafs all their movements: and if they fhould be fuch as to cover them from the approach of the enemy, to the attack, they will equally prevent their moving forward

to

to meet them, but the enemy's artillery, and infantry, will be enabled to advance againſt them without danger, and by their fire oblige them to quit their poſition, without having it in their power to take their revenge.

It is almoſt impoſſible that cavalry, who would act agreeable to the principles of that arm, and move forward to the charge of an enemy to be attacked, ſhould be able to preſerve an apui capable of covering their flanks for any time ; for it will rarely, if ever happen, that the protecting object, whatever it may be, hollow way, moraſs, &c. which might happen to cover them in their poſition of formation, will extend up to the poſition on which they muſt march to the attack ; this was experienced in particular at Prague, where our right was protected by a piece of water, when we formed for the attack, but which was quitted and left in our rear, ſo ſoon as we advanced : and the enemy taking the advantage of that circumſtance, attacked our advancing wing in flank ; and had it not been for a ſudden and unpremeditated manœuvre, our cavalry, which was deranged by it, would not have been enabled to rally again during the remainder of the action, notwithſtanding he followed up his advantage, with too much caution and ſlowneſs.

Natural obſtacles therefore, are not, in all caſes, to be depended upon, for the protection of the flanks of cavalry ; and it muſt be conſidered what other means can be made uſe of for that purpoſe.

When the infantry were encamped in the centre, and cavalry on the wings, the King of Pruſſia always placed ſome battalions of grenadiers upon the exterior flanks of the cavalry, fronting outwards to cloſe the line, but which, as ſoon as the army prepared

for

SECURITY OF THE FLANKS.

FIG. 1.   *Page* 52.

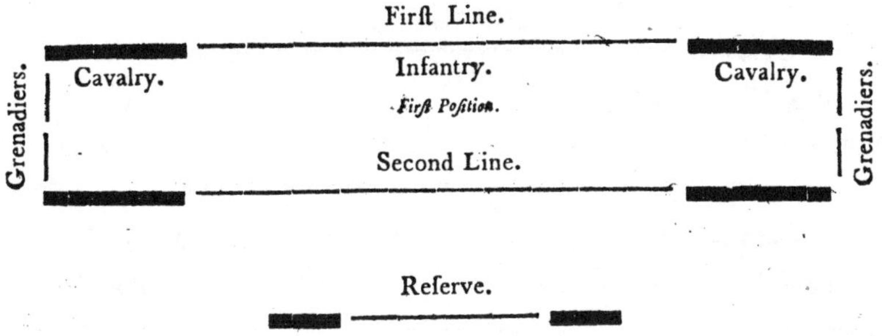

First Line.

Grenadiers. | Cavalry.   Infantry.   Cavalry. | Grenadiers.

First Position.

Second Line.

Reserve.

FIG. 2.   *Page* 53.

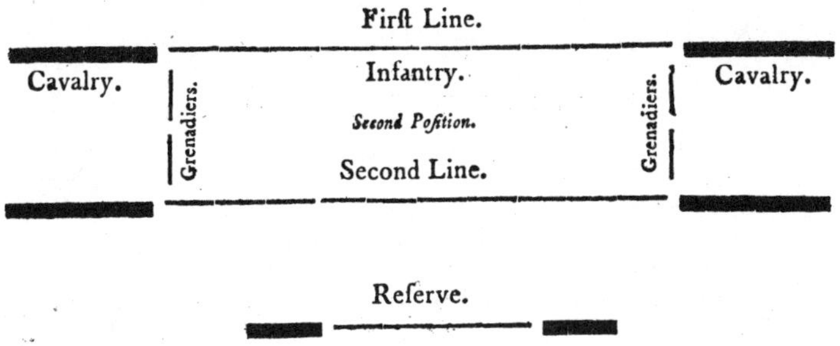

First Line.

Cavalry.   Grenadiers. | Infantry.   *Second Position.* | Grenadiers.   Cavalry.

Second Line.

Reserve.

FIG. 3.

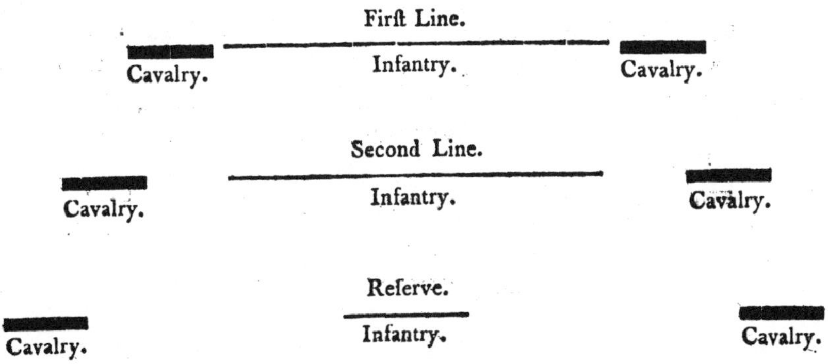

First Line.

Cavalry.   Infantry.   Cavalry.

Second Line.

Cavalry.   Infantry.   Cavalry.

Reserve.

Cavalry.   Infantry.   Cavalry.

SECURITY OF FLANKS.

FIG. 1.

Page 54.

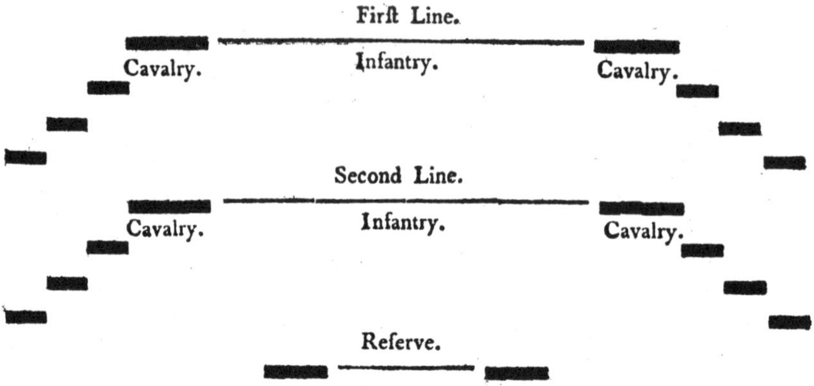

First Line.

Cavalry.   Infantry.   Cavalry.

Second Line.

Cavalry.   Infantry.   Cavalry.

Reserve.

FIG. 2.

Page 54.

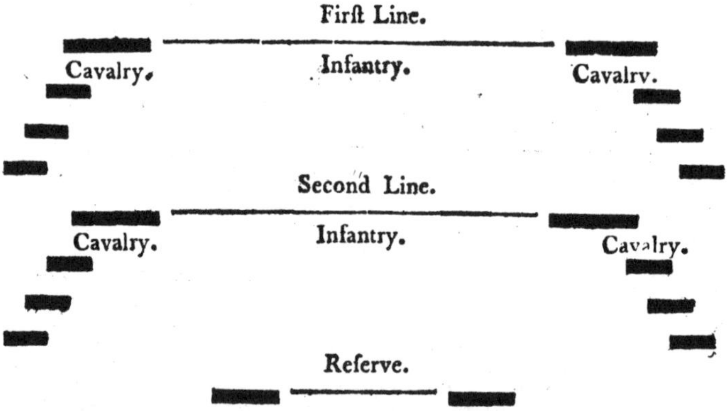

First Line.

Cavalry.   Infantry.   Cavalry.

Second Line.

Cavalry.   Infantry.   Cavalry.

Reserve.

for action, in an open country, went to the right about, and joined the flank of the infantry; the army thus formed a long fquare. The advantages of this difpofition are, firft in checking, and ftopping the enemy's cavalry, fhould yours be repulfed and purfued; which a well fupported fire by thefe battalions, upon the flank of the purfuing enemy, cannot fail to effect, the inftant their own have paffed along their front, who will be enabled to rally under the protection of this fire, and follow up the enemy in their turn. This happened to the Pruffians, at Collin : and to the Auftrians, at Leuthen. It is faid, that in the firft-mentioned battle, this manœuvre was formed fuddenly upon the fpot: but at Leuthen, the King formed his upon mature deliberation, made previous to the engagement.

The fecond advantage is, preventing your own cavalry, if defeated, from retreating between the two lines of infantry of the army for protection, which they are very apt to do in great confufion, where the enemy will not fail to follow, and might endanger throwing them into diforder, and caufe the defeat of the whole army.

Other difpofitions or orders of battle, which might be formed for the protection of the flanks of cavalry, agreeable to the circumftances, or nature of the ground, are,

Firft. The flank of the firft line, being covered by the fecond, extending a certain diftance beyond, or outflanking it, in fuch manner, that any troops, who would attack the flank of that line, muft themfelves prefent a flank to this: and this fecond line to be in like manner covered by the referve, outflanking it; the contrary has been the moft general practice, without any fufficient reafon.

P   *Second*

Second. Some fquadrons might be placed upon the flanks, in inter-line, at 100 or 150 paces in the rear of each, and to extend beyond the flanks the whole length of their front. Thefe will proteƈt the flanks of their refpeƈtive lines: and can manœuvre feparately, as occafion may require, either by wheeling outwards to front any fquadrons of the enemy, which might have made a circuit to fall upon the flanks of the pofition, or by moving forward to extend the line, as light horfe.

Third. A few fquadrons of Huffars, may be placed in column, upon each wing, to form an echellon; each fquadron to extend beyond the outward flank of the preceding one, about half its front; from this dif-pofition, they are ready to deploy, in an inftant, up into line, or by wheeling outwards, until their flanks communicate, and form an oblique line outwards from each flank; or they can, in an inftant, form a column to move rapidly forward, and wheel upon the flanks of the enemy, either during the attack, or preparatory to it.

Fourth and *laƒt* method is, for a corps of light horfe to be entirely detached from the line, and pofted in the rear, to aƈt as circumftances might render neceffary for the proteƈtion of the flank, to which his at-tention is particularly direƈted; the operations of this corps muft be entrufted entirely to the judgment and experience cf the officer who commands it, who ought to be a man of quick perception, and rapid execution. He will fometimes find the moft effeƈtual manner of pro-teƈting the flank of his own lines, will be by attacking thofe of the enemy; fhould the wing to which he belongs, make a fuccefsful charge, he will direƈtly pafs before it in purfuit of the defeated enemy.

By

By thofe, and other difpofitions, which will frequently occur to an officer of experience, in the courfe of fervice, cavalry might be fo placed as to protect and cover their own flanks, and render it impracticable for an enemy, without great rifk, to attack them, even with a great fuperiority, and in a country devoid of all chicane.

A relation of the occurrences that took place at the battle of Prague, in which the author bore a part, will illuftrate the above reflections, and evince the utility of fuch difpofitions.

The left wing of our cavalry was apuied upon a large piece of water, which for the time fecured that flank, and made it a good defenfive pofition for infantry. General Haddick, who commanded the wing oppofed to us, formed his Huffars en potence, extending beyond the piece of water, which did not reach above an hundred yards in our front, in fuch manner, that in advancing we muft march directly into this potence, and expofe our flank to thofe Huffars, to counteract thefe, five fquadrons were placed in column, in interline upon that flank : but this was badly judged, fince in quitting the water they could not deploy or form, but by giving their flanks in fucceffion to the Huffars of Haddick ; it was however neceffary to move forward, the lines being in motion for that purpofe : The author was pofted in the rear of the left of the infantry, with five fquadrons of Huffars, to act as circumftances might require, who, before the attack commenced, rode with General Norman, to the front, to obferve the difpofitions that were making, and the pofition of the enemy ; the error above alluded to, was quickly perceived, and the author propofed to General Norman, who commanded the fecond line, to order fome fquadrons of dragoons to wheel to the right, and march round the piece of water, to attack, in flank, this potence of Huffars

fo

fo regularly formed to enclofe and furround our left, as foon as it fhould move 100 paces forward; that General hefitated, and did not think he was authorifed to make fuch a movement of his own anthority, or from fome other reafon. On rejoining the five fquadrons, and after having explained, in a few words, to the officers of it, the reafons for making that movement, the author commanded to the left by files, and on the march to extend the front, reduced the three ranks into two, and likewife formed large intervals between the fquadrons. The water was now on our right; General Haddick obferved this manœuvre, and as he had abundance of Huffars, he detached eight fquadrons to counteract it, without in the leaft deranging his potence. Thefe two hoftile corps having paffed the pond, approached each other in parallel lines, very clofe together, and each redoubled their pace to gain the flank of the other; our fquadrons aimed at their right, and they at our left. In the mean time our cavalry in line charged, and were at firft fo far fuccefsful as to overfet almoft all the enemy's firft line; they were however afterwards in their turn repulfed and obliged to retreat, which was very much to be attributed to the attack of thofe Huffars en potence upon the flank. Haddicks Huffars having our fquadrons on their left, made a difcharge with their carbines, without halting; however, no perfon was touched by it, though we were not 100 paces diftant; our fquadrons, having got fafter over the ground than they did, outflanked them, at length by half a fquadron; fronted, charged, and difperfed them, and two fquadrons were detached in their purfuit. The pond, which by this time we had nearly marched round, was ftill on our right, the three remaining fquadrons were wheeled to the right, and by that manœuvre hemmed in feveral troops of Haddick's Huffars, which had paffed through the large intervals, and who inftantly furrendered, and with them we re-took feveral of ours they had taken. Our fquadrons then

formed,

FIG. 1.

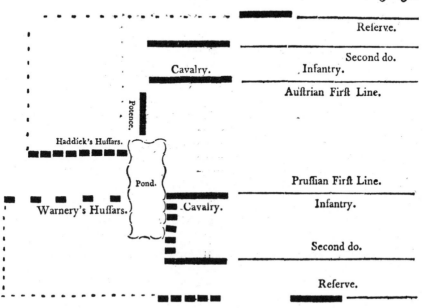

Reserve.

Second do.

Cavalry.

Infantry.

Austrian First Line.

Potence.

Haddick's Hussars.

Pond.

Pruffian First Line.

Warnery's Hussars.

Cavalry.

Infantry.

Second do.

Reserve.

FIG. 2.

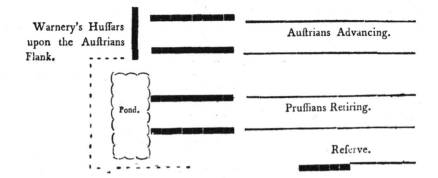

Warnery's Hussars
upon the Austrians
Flank.

Austrians Advancing.

Pond.

Pruffians Retiring.

Reserve.

Flankers.

Flankers.

Huffars.

Dragoons.

Grenadiers.

Dragoons.

ADVANCED GUARD.

Grenadiers.

Cavalry.

Infantry.

formed, completed the tour of the water, and marched upon the right flank of the Auftrian cavalry, which followed ours too leifurly, though not in much order. At the appearance of thofe fquadrons upon their flank, they immediately halted; thefe were the horfe grenadiers of Purpurati, who on this demonftration againft their flank, by no more, at this time, than 200 Huffars; (the furplus being occupied in taking prifoners, collecting horfes, &c.) advanced not a ftep farther.

The King of Pruffia approved of this manœuvre, and juft before the battle of Colin, the author being on his return with 700 horfe, from a patrole, which he had been making up to the mouth of the Saftova, in Moldau, was met by the King, who faid, that as he had fo much contributed to the fecurity of the flank of the army, at the battle of Prague, he would expect the fame fervice from him here; for which purpofe he fhould retain the command of the detachment, at prefent with him, and act on the left as he might fee occafion. Though this was certaiuly an honourable teftimony of the author's fervice, yet he hopes the relation of it will not be attributed to vanity: but as an inftance of the utility of detached corps, to act as occafion might require; having a pointed and determined object, fuch as that, in the prefent cafe, for the protection of the flanks.

Q

CHAP

C H A P. VI.

Of the March, and the Deploy.

EVERY corps of cavalry, of whatever magnitude, or at any time in peace, as well as war; and in all fituations, as well at home as abroad, fhould on all occafions, have on a march, an advance, and an arrear guard; and always where practicable fmall patroles, or flankers, upon equal front with them, detached to the right and left, more or lefs, according to the nature of the ground; they muft afcend the heights near them, that they may be enabled to difcover the furrounding country, examine the roads, villages, open country, woods, &c. and inftantly report every thing extraordinary which they may obferve, fuch as troops in motion, fignals, &c. However unneceffary this might appear, when there is no apprehenfions of an enemy, yet it is a very important inftruction, both to officers and foldiers, and habituates them to vigilance; and troops who have been accuftomed to take thefe precautions in time of peace, it will certainly be very difficult to furprife, in the operations of actual fervice in the neighbourhood of an enemy.

Several military authors have employed their pens in the detail of meafures to be taken for the fecurity of the march of troops, which is indeed an important object, as well for night marches, as thofe by day; Birac, in particular, has treated on the former.

An

An army on its march towards the enemy, either to take an advantageous pofition nearer to that occupied by him, or with the intent of attacking him in it, muft always be preceded by a ftrong advanced guard, compofed of infantry, and cavalry; at prefent the corps of referve is generally felected for that fervice, becaufe they are compofed of grenadiers, and other chofen and refolute troops, prepared for every enterprize. This advance guard fhould move forward, before the army, and occupy fuch pofitions, paffes, or defilés, as might happen to be on or near the line of march of the columns of the army, and poft themfelves in fuch a manner, as to be enabled to maintain fuch pofitions againft all the attacks of the enemy, until the arrival of their own army.

Let us fuppofe the operations of the army to lay in a plain and open country; and that it is to march forward by the right, in eight columns, each line forming four; thofe of the fecond line following the rear of the firft. On approaching the pofition or emplacement, where they are to reform the order of battle; the heads of the columns of the fecond line, difengage themfelves to the right of the rear divifions of the firft, and move forward, until the cavalry arrive at the fixth fquadron from the front, upon which they continue to regulate their march, until the fquadrons clofe forward to deploy. See the plan.

The

The propriety and correctnefs of this manœuvre, a little inveftigation will make evident: for if the columns of the fecond line were to remain attached to the rear of thofe of the firft, until the fignal was given for the army to deploy into line; fhould thofe columns be ftrong, they would have a confiderable diftance to march in column after the firft had deployed, before they would arrive upon the ground on which they were to form; as they could not begin to move until the column of that line had quitted their ground: or fhould they begin to deploy at the fame time with the firft, the fecond line would be formed at too great a diftance from the other, and muft either march forward in line, or break into columns for that purpofe, both of which are fubject to much confufion and lofs of time, befides other confiderable inconveniences which muft, if poffible, be always avoided in prefence of an enemy.

But by the heads of the columns of the fecond line, difengaging to the right, or left, according to the wing by which the army marched off their ground; and to that which they are confequently to deploy, and moving up to the battalion or fquadron, that correfponds to the diftance between the two lines which we here fuppofed to be the fixth; upon the fignal to deploy being given, the whole army, firft and fecond, lines, (and the referve, by the fame means) begin to deploy in the fame time, and all immediately form up to their proper places, and diftances; the fquadrons of the fecond line oppofite to the intervals of thofe of the firft.

A column of troops of any number of fquadrons, by whatever flank they may have been broken into column might deploy on the right, left, or centre, or any intermediate fquadrons; this may be better ex-

plained

plained by fmall pieces of cards numbered to reprefent the fquadrons; in whatever manner the fquadrons are to deploy, they ought always to march upon a given point of fupport, or appui.

Whenever an army is to make a movement or manœuvre in columns, the heads of them ought to regulate their march by each other, both as to line and diflance, as much as the nature of the ground will permit, fo that on an alarm, in the fhorteft time poffible the whole may deploy into line, in their natural pofitions, without hurry or confufion: The heads of the columns fhould march with the ordinary ftep, that the fucceeding divifions might be enabled to preferve their diftances without hurrying, which moft frequently happens from the negligence of the officers; a fingle perfon ftopping a moment in front of a troop to light his pipe, or any other reafon, is fufficient to derange the order of the march of the whole column; they move on brifkly to regain their diftance, which every fucceeding divifion is obliged to do, in an increafed proportion. The ftriftelt attention fhould be paid to that circumftance.

When a defilé, or other obftacle, is to be paffed, the leading divifions fhould move very flow, until the rear of the column has paffed it, and then the ordinary pace infenfibly refumed.

A column of cavalry, on its march towards the enemy, before they arrive within the range of cannon fhot, fhould make the divifions, or quarter fquadrons clofe up forward; the officers, and non-commiffioned officers, who are not pofted in the ranks, move to the flanks, that nothing might prevent the divifion from clofing well upon the leading one; care muft be taken to avoid confufion: and that the

R

fquadrons,

fquadrons, and battalions, do not intermix, but remain at ten paces
from each other : The word, *form fquadron,* is then given, which is
to be performed in the manner defcribed in the books of exercife, and
is in general every where fimilar; this muft be done with quicknefs and
precifion: the rear divifions, upon the oblique, at a gallop; the whole
continue the march at the ordinary pace, and clofe the fquadrons forward, within 12 paces of each other; (in this manner 30 fquadrons
does not appear at a diftance to be more than ten, marching with their
open diftances ; advantage of which may frequently be taken to deceive
an enemy, as to the ftrength of a column, efpecially when the ftandards
are lowered for that purpofe) but here it is meant to facilitate the rapidity and correctnefs of the deploying into line, and to prevent the
horfes of the rear fquadrons from having too far to gallop, from thence
to the oppofite extremity of the line or wing to which they belong,
and frequently over interfecting valleys, ditches, &c. whereas this
clofe formation brings them nearly upon the ground of their pofition,
and prevents their being galloped out of wind to get into line before
the action commences.

By the means above defcribed, a Pruffian army of any magnitude,
muft be formed in order of battle, in eight minutes, commencing from
the inftant that the fignal is given to deploy, provided the number of
columns are proportioned to the ftrength of the army.

At Leuthen, the King of Pruffia did not make the army deploy,
although it advanced in feveral columns. When the heads of the columns of the army had arrived within fight of the right wing of Prince
Charles of Lorain's army, where they made their appearance, on purpofe to deceive him, as to the point of attack, and which caufed General

Luchezy

Plate 20.*

Oblique line.

First Manœuvre

Luchezy, who commanded that wing to demand the referve; all the heads of the columns wheeled at once to the right obliquely, and marched forward until they joined the rear of the right hand column, which was their natural order of battle, having marched by the right; thus, in an inftant, the whole army, without quitting the ordinary ftep, where formed, by a quarter wheel to the left, by divifions, into an oblique line, upon the enemy's left wing, before they had time to make any movement to interrupt, or difpofition to counteract that manœuvre.

Another order of march towards the enemy is, by the flank, in order of battle; the whole army, firft and fecond line, and referve, wheeling to the right or left, by divifions, each forming a feparate column; and when arrived upon the ground, upon which they are to re-form, they have nothing to do but to wheel oppofite flanks into line : or upon the fame backwards, which will be more correct, as the pivots will all be preferved, and cover.

This was the order of march of the King of Pruffia's army, at the battle of Prague, and at Collin, having marched by the left; and in feveral other battles likewife.

Reichenberg was the only battle in which the Pruffians formed by deploying, and there without any very good reafon; the author has made feveral obfervations upon that battle in another work. The whole of the forming and manœuvring performed in that action, was different from what is ufually practifed; the cavalry was formed and engaged in the centre, and the infantry on the right. At Torgou,

the

the corps commanded by the King marched off by the left: and that of Zeithen, by the right.

This manner of marching by lines, is the only one which ought to be made ufe of on marching parallel to the enemy, becaufe the line is formed to its proper front, in an inftant, if the enemy fhould make any demonftrations of attacking it upon its march.

To mention fomething further relative to the deployment, fuppofe five fquadrons to have formed column by the right, on their march, are commanded to deploy; at the word of command, the fifth or laft fquadron continues to march forward, the others march obliquely to the right, by traverfing; but if the columns fhould be ftronger, then the leading divifions fhould wheel to the right, and march upon the point of appui, until they arrive at their pofition in the line, and then front into it.

The commanding officers of the fquadrons which deploy to the right, look to the left, though the reft of the fquadron keep their eyes to the right becaufe they muft drefs upon the fifth fquadron, which is thus performed: fo foon as the fourth fquadron, by traverfing to the right, has cleared the front of the fifth, and has taken its interval of 20 or 25 paces, the officer commands, *halt; eyes to the left; drefs;* the third fquadron performs the fame by the fourth; and thus in fucceffion, until the whole are formed, and dreffed by the fifth fquadron. The commanding officer of the regiment then gives the word, *eyes to the right;* and *drefs;* they are then to regulate their movements by the right hand fquadron; which becomes the fquadron of direction.

To

Plate 21. ✳

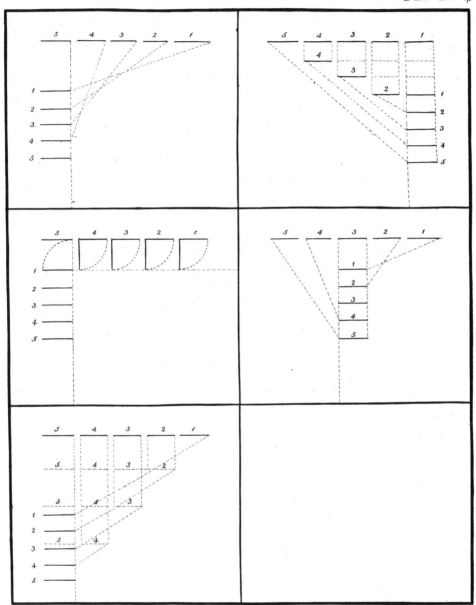

Second Manœuvre

To deploy to the left, which is more eafy than to the right, the leading or right hand fquadron moves flowly forward, their eyes to the right, other fquadrons, eyes to the left, except the commanding officers; the fecond fquadron traverfes to the left, and forms line with the firft, which the commanding officer obferving, commands, *eyes to the right; drefs;* thefe continue to move forward, and the third traverfes into line the fame, and thus in fucceffion, until the whole are formed; or having formed column by the right, they are to deploy upon the centre. Then the third fquadron muft continue to move forward : the two firft fquadrons muft traverfe to the right, and the rear ones to the left, as in the two preceding examples. The centre fquadron being in this manœuvre, that of direction, the two firft drefs eyes to the left, and the two rear fquadrons to the right; and vice verfa fhould the column have marched by the left.

By being attentive that the Colonel's right hand fquadron always forms to the right of the line, no miftake or confufion can ever happen, provided a proper degree of attention is paid, by both officers and troopers, to the aids above defcribed.

S

CHAP.

C H A P. VII.

Of gaining the Flank of an Enemy.

AFTER having provided for the fafety of the flanks of his own army, the principal attention of a General, in the time of action, ought to be how to fucceed in gaining thofe of his enemy; this is a very important operation, or rather decifive, but very difficult to perform, and only to be attempted by troops who have been accuftomed to manœuvre with great order and precifion, as well as rapidity and fpirit, and muft be fo fuddenly performed, as not to allow the enemy time to form his counter difpofitions, to interrupt them, or even to difcover the intention, but in the moment of its execution.

The moft fimple manner of gaining an enemy's flank, is by extending the front, until it exceeds the length of that occupied by them, which is called outflanking: but few officers will be fo fimple as not to obferve it, and muft be very weak indeed, not to devife means to punifh thofe who adopt it. A fecond and much preferable method is, at the moment the line moves forward to the attack, the two flank fquadrons detach themfelves from it, and wheel the half circle by divifions, and march with rapidity upon the flank of the enemy's lines.

The King of Pruffia performed this manœuvre, by making the leading fquadron move forward to the enemy's fecond line, and to attack
that in flank at the fame time that the others fell upon that of the firft,
or at leaft to make fuch demonftration, as to prevent that line from
moving forward to extricate the flank of the other : by this manœuvre,
the fquadron, which has gained the flank of the firft line, is protected
by the leading fquadron, from being attacked itfelf in flank, by that of
the fecond; and if the enemy has not made his previous difpofitions to
counteract fuch attack, his defeat will be certain, before the referve can
be brought up to remedy it; fuch operations as thofe are generally
finifhed in a few minutes, being followed up by the charge of the whole
wing in almoft the fame inftant.

Two other fquadrons might be concealed in the rear of the line, to
fupply the place of thofe who quit it to fall upon the enemy's flank,
the moment they move forward for that purpofe, this would prevent
that wing from being weakened by their abfence: but great care
muft be taken that nothing which might tend to an indication of fuch
preparation may be difcovered by the enemy, as that would defeat its
effect.

This manœuvre is fubject to caution, and can only be performed with
light active cavalry accuftomed to move with rapidity, order, and preciffion, commanded by brave, intelligent, and decided officers.

A third method of gaining an enemy's flank, is by forming a column of
light cavalry upon the extremity of each wing in interline, as if intended for the fecurity of that flank; each of thofe columns may be
compofed of a regiment of cavalry, and are to move forward in column

by

by divifions, at full gallop, and when arrived at the height of the enemy's flank, the divifions wheel to the right or left, into line, without halting, and charge in the fame time that the line moves forward to the attack in front. If a regiment fhould thus fucceed in gaining an enemy's flank, the operation is foon finifhed : for one fquadron, in fuch a moment, charging as abovementioned, is fufficient to decide the fuccefs of the attack of a whole wing, and even the fate of a battle.

Or two or three fquadrons of the head of the column might deploy to mafk the manœuvre, and cover the flanks of the reft of the column, on its movement, to the enemy's flank, as might be thought moft expedient according to the nature of the ground, troops, and other circumftances.

Cavalry ought for this purpofe to be frequently exercifed to trot and gallop in column, without lofing their diftances ; that at the word, *halt, front,* or *wheel into line ;* the whole may be at once formed, and ready to charge forward.

A column fhould frequently practice moving upon irregular and curve lines, zig zags, and angles, which is difficult to perform in order, but frequently neceffary in the field ; and above all, at the word *trot,* or *gallop,* fhould break immediately into that pace, and continue in it with a regular and uniform movement, until another word of command is given; this in a great meafure depends upon the attention of the officers. With a wing or corps of cavalry, accuftomed to fuch precifion in all their movements, the moft daring and hazardous enterprizes might be attempted with fuccefs, as they are at all times

ready

Plate 22 ✳

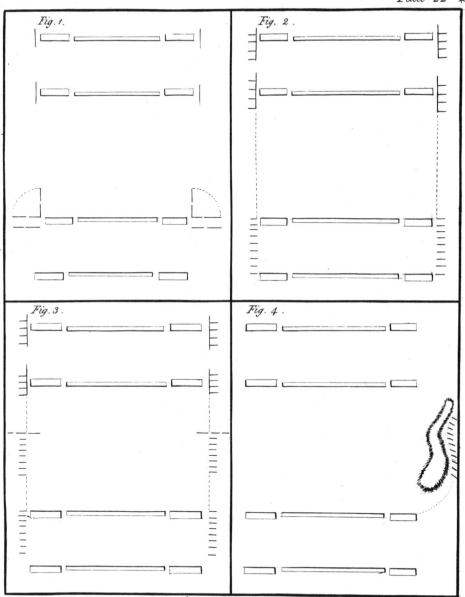

Fig. 1.

Fig. 2.

Fig. 3.

Fig. 4.

Third Manœuvre

ready for action, and find it equally practicable to attack an enemy at a critical moment of weaknefs or diforder, or avoid him when fuperior.

It was with fuch troops as thofe above aluded to, that Seydlitz decided the fuccefs of the battle of Rofback, taking the advantage of the ground, by making the circuit of a rideau which was favourable for it, he mafked the movement which he made with the dragoons to fall upon the enemy's flank; who did not perceive them until the moment they were attacked.

Sometimes an enemy's flank is gained by a corps of light cavalry, concealed at hand, to fall upon it at the moment that the line moves forward to the charge; the Auftrian Huffars had this advantage at the battle of Sohr, but loft it by pillaging the baggage. They were fuppofed to be then under the command of Werner, afterwards a Lieutenant General in the Pruffian fervice.

When an army abounds in light cavalry, a part of them might be very ufefully employed in making a circuit during the action, to form a demonftration of attack, in the rear of the enemy's line, and on their flank; being careful to make their tour fo wide, as not to fall in with any enemy's pofts, or parties, to avoid difcovery.

The appearance of fuch troops in the enemy's rear, during the engagement, cannot fail to have a very important effect, and will not fubject fuch detachment to any very great rifk, even if they fhould not fucceed: for light cavalry, commanded by an enterprifing officer, if they fhould be intercepted on one fide, will always be enabled to retire

T

by

by the other, or extricate themfelves in a hundred different manners A good light cavalry, well conducted, can never be cut off, nor fail of accomplifhing their retreat. This manœuvre was frequently performed by the troops of the King of Pruffia.

———————

C H A P. VIII.

Distribution of Cavalry, in the Line, and Corps de Reserve; and the Disposition of that Arm opposed to Infantry.

IT would much conduce to the ftrength of a pofition, if all the infantry of an army were encamped in the firft and fecond lines, and the cavalry in the rear of them; they are certainly very improper for the flanks of a permanent or defencive pofition, and are utterly defencelefs in night attacks or furprifes, and require both artillery and infantry to protect them. It is furprifing that opportunities have not more frequently been taken to punifh thofe who encamp in this defective, though ufual manner.

Infantry, by the nature of its arms and inftitution is enabled to defend itfelf in every fituation, and on all natures of ground, which cavalry cannot do, and therefore fhould not be expofed to be attacked upon its own ground; but being fecured from furprife or fudden attack

by

by the infantry in its front; by the rapidity of its movement, is enabled inſtantly to render itſelf at its poſt on the wings, or wherever it might happen to be aſſigned, before an enemy can have made any progreſs, and will find the ground on which it is to act unincumbered by tents, forage, or any other impediment; many other advantages accruing from this diſpoſition will immediately ſtrike an experienced officer, and which it will therefore be needleſs here to ennumerate.

The advanced guards of the cavalry ſhould, notwithſtanding, extend along the front of the poſition, and on its flanks, and rear; and the cavalry ſhould have their poſts correctly aſſigned them, upon which they might move in the ſhorteſt time poſſible, after an alarm or ſignal has been given for that purpoſe.

Count St. Germain, in his manœuvres, is of the ſame opinion with regard to the encamping of cavalry, as every officer muſt be, who re-flects ſeriouſly upon the nature of that arm. A camp ought to reſem-ble a fortreſs, and cavalry is acknowledged not to be proper for the defenſive.

Cavalry has frequently been encamped in the manner above recom-mended, but upon broken and interſected ground only, which would not admit of its being in the firſt line; for inſtance, in the poſition on which the army were encamped, before the battle of Roſback, in con-ſequence of a ravine extending along the front of the army: ſo ſoon as the troops moved forward to the attack, the cavalry filed off to the left, and formed two lines; the regiments which belonged to the right wing, forming the ſecond; by which diſpoſition all the cavalry of the army, except the grand guards, were formed on the left of the infantry.

Before

Before the battle of Lobofchitz, the Pruffian cavalry was formed in the front of the centre of the infantry, but that was becaufe a thick fog prevented that army from difcovering the movements of that of the enemy commanded by General Brown, which were thought to be retrograde, and it was therefore imagined that this would be nothing but an attack of the rear guard.

At Zornfdorf all the cavalry were placed in the rear of the infantry, and did not come into action until after their defeat; Seydlitz, who had never hitherto particularly diftinguifhed himfelf, did not think that the cavalry which was under his command, ought to retire at fo cheap a rate, and fucceeded fo well in the manœuvres which he performed with it, as to reftore the fuccefs of the action, at a time when it was conceived to be irretrieveable, and nothing thought of but how to fecure the beft retreat.

Every General commanding an army, at the commencement of a campaign, forms a plan or arrangement of the difpofition of the troops under his command, diftributing them into brigades, wings, firft and fecond lines, referves, corps of obfervation, communication, &c. and this difpofition is called the order of battle; but it is not to be imagined that it is literally adhered to on all occafions in prefence of an enemy; the real intention of it is to determine the rank and fituation of the General officers to the command of infantry, cavalry, centre and wings of the army of the firft and fecond lines, referve, &c. as well as of regiments, brigades, divifions, &c. all of which muft be accurately fettled, and clearly underftood, before the army begins to move, to prevent confufion and diffatisfaction amongft the troops and officers.

This

This order of battle, is that in which the army would encamp in a plain and open country, for the purpose of a review, or when under no apprehensions of an enemy : but by no means binding to the General commanding the army, to abide by on all occasions, as such dispositions must be combined by him as corresponds to the nature of the ground, situation of the enemy, and the kind of service to be performed by the army ; whether upon the offensive or defensive : and various other reasons, which depend entirely upon the judgment and decision of the General, agreeable to the object of the campaign.

Every detached corps, of any considerable strength, should always have its order of battle; of which each officer of the staff ought to have a copy.

The corps de reserve is at present frequently composed in the same manner as a piquet : but we will here suppose it such as it ought to be, composed of infantry, and cavalry, appointed to perform that particular service, and under the command of such officers as are best acquainted with the nature and importance of it. Sometimes the corps de reserve is composed according to the nature of the ground, of cavalry only. Light cavalry is the most proper to be employed on this service, by reason of the advantage they possess of being enabled to render themselves, with promptness and expedition, to any part of the line, which might be particularly pressed upon by the enemy, and begin to give way ; every thing depends upon their arriving with alacrity in this critical moment; it is certain, much more depends upon that circumstance, than even the effect of their attack when arrived, and therefore those Generals who have placed cuirassiers in their corps de reserve, had not good reason for so doing.

U

The

The moft advantageous difpofition with regard to the referve, is to divide it into three diftinct corps, one to be placed in the rear of each wing of infantry, and the third in the rear of the centre of the fecond line: but the King of Pruffia, from fcarcity of troops to oppofe the numerous armies he had to engage, was frequently obliged to have only the latter, and even that to confift of Huffars only, to which a battalion frank or two were fometimes added.

A corps de referve is of fuch importance, that no army, corps, or detachment of troops, however fmall, fhould be without one proportioned to their ftrength; the advantage of having troops at hand, to correct any error or defect in the lines of an army, at the moment of attack, is evidently very important; for inftance: Suppofe the line to have moved forward upon falfe points, and confequently to break in many places, this defect would continually increafe, and rifk the defeat of the army, were it not for the referve; a few battalions, or fquadrons of which, marching into that interval, immediately remedies it.

It is likewife neceffary to have troops in referve, to fupport any part of the line, againft which the principal efforts of the enemy might happen to be directed; or to relieve any regiment whofe ranks might have been fo much thinned during the action, as to weaken the line in that part. Alfo to check the progrefs of an enemy, who may have penetrated the line before he has time to take the full advantage of his fuccefs; and nothing tends more to reftore the exertions and confidence of troops, who might happen to be particularly preffed upon by the enemy, than the arrival of frefh troops from the referve, to their fupport: and confequently, nothing tends more to abate the ardour of the enemy. And laftly, the utility of the referve is very great, to fecure the retreat of the army, when after every effort, the fate of the day has been unfavourable.

favourable. Inftances of the advantages of each of thofe applica-
tions of the referve have been too frequent, in all times and
fervices, to render it neceffary to particularize any of them to a
military reader.

The referve likewife ferves to accelerate the defeat of an
enemy, by advancing rapidly upon their infantry fo foon as it appears
to be ready to give way; this the regiment of Bayreuth performed at Strigau; or to charge the troops who cover the retreat
of a defeated enemy, when the infantry cannot come up with them;
which diftinction muft be underftood; for the difference is very great,
between an attack by cavalry againft infantry, frefh, and in good order,
formed, and prepared to receive it: and that of falling upon thofe
who are covering a retreat, after their army has been defeated.
It is however fometimes abfolutely neceffary for cavalry to attack infantry perfectly in order, and prepared for their reception; the
following is a difpofition for that purpofe, which the author himfelf
has practifed, on more than one occafion, with fuccefs.

Suppofe a corps of referve to be compofed of fifteen fquadrons,
five of which are dragoons, and the remainder Huffars: The whole muft
pafs through the lines of their infantry at the fame time, intervals being
formed for that purpofe, by doubling the ranks. The firft five fquadrons
form column, the ten others form line, upon the right and left of the
rear fquadron of the column of dragoons: the column fhould clofe
up without however mixing or confounding the fquadrons; the
whole muft move forward together; the dragoons, with the greateft
vivacity, throw themfelves upon the enemy's infantry, fword in hand,
at the fame time making loud huzzas, and fcreams: The remaining ten
fquadrons

fquadrons advance with lefs rapidity, and in good order, having little more to do, until the column has penetrated, than to protect it againft any attack of the enemy's cavalry, and to prevent the infantry from forming flanks againft them.

The column muft obferve, firft to remain well clofed, rather in mafs than open, to increafe the weight of their charge, and to form a lefs object for the enemy's fire, of which the ten others, however attract alfo their proportion. Secondly, they fhould always give loud huzzas, or fcreams, in the attack of infantry, to alarm and confound them, as well as to prevent their own horfes and men from hearing the whiftling of the balls, the found of which, on fuch an occafion, intimidates more than the effect of them; this is the reafon why that difference is to be made between the attack of infantry and cavalry, which latter muft be charged with the greateft order, and as much filence as poffible, that all the words of command, and fignals of the trumpet, may be diftinctly heard: without that, all would foon be confufion; but the cafe is totally different in the attack of infantry; in charging of which, it is allowed by all officers of cavalry, to be very effential for the troopers to emit loud fcreams or huzzas. The author of thefe remarks, without this, perhaps would not have fucceeded as he did near Schandau, in 1756, in totally deftroying the Auftrian grenadiers, under the command of Loudon, at that time Lieutenant Colonel; notwithftanding the obftinate defence they bravely made; and this was performed with only 450 Huffars. The manœuvres, and courageous refiftance made by thofe brave croat grenadiers, where fuch as to merit the greateft praife, and infpire refpect for that nation; though under fuch a commanding officer, they could hardly do other than acquire reputation.

The

Plate 23. *

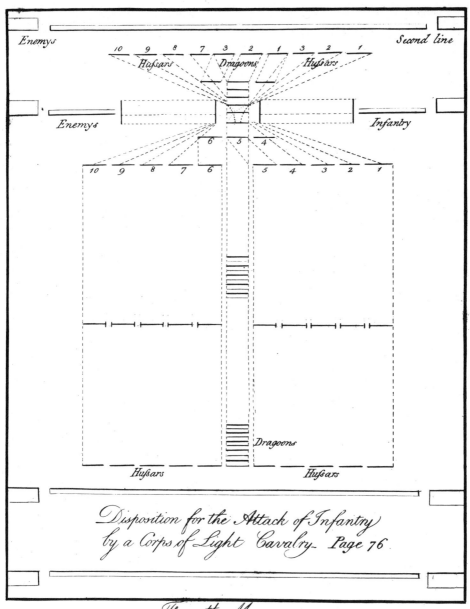

Disposition for the Attack of Infantry
by a Corps of Light Cavalry— Page 76.

Fourth Manœuvre

The column of dragoons muſt advance in as cloſe order as poſſible; the officers, and non-commiſſioned officers on the flanks, and thoſe who cloſe the rear of the column, muſt prevent the troopers from quitting it, either on the flanks or rear, and ſhould not even omit to do ſo with the ſword or piſtol, if other means in this trying moment ſhould not be ſufficient; ſimple words will be of no avail with ſome ſoldiers, and no time muſt now be loſt in altercation.

The three firſt ſquadrons having pierced and paſſed through the ene-my's firſt line, move forward and deploy in front of the ſecond line, or the reſerve; the fourth wheels to the right, and the fifth to the left, to roll up the infantry, by the flanks which the firſt has opened. The ten ſquadrons of Huſſars which follow, will prevent the enemy from making any movement to interrupt this operation; with a well diſ-ciplined, active, and reſolute corps of cavalry, this is much ſooner performed than deſcribed: and completed before the enemy will have time to bring up his reſerve to counteract it. A firſt line of infantry being thus, or by any other means broken, and diſperſed, the ſecond is uſually defeated without much difficulty: becauſe they cannot make uſe of their fire arms without killing the diſperſed ſoldiers of their own firſt line: not to mention the confuſion and diſmay, which muſt natu-rally prevail under ſuch circumſtances. Of the ten ſquadrons of Huſſars, ſeven ſhould then paſs through, and form in line with the three ſquadrons of dragoons, to oppoſe the enemy's ſecond line or reſerve: but if there ſhould be no apprehenſions of that line, or the enemy's cavalry, either from their being at too great a diſtance, or any other reaſon, then the whole fifteen ſquadrons might act againſt the infantry; it was nearly in this manner that Seydlitz manœuvred at Zornſdorf; Marſhal Geſler,

X   at at Strigau; and General Leideritz, at Keffelfdorf; where no cavalry appeared to difengage their infantry who were thus roughly handled.

This manœuvre, however, is fubject to very great caution, provided the enemy's cavalry fhould be at hand, to fall upon the dragoons whilft fabring the infantry, unlefs they fhould be fuch as might be fafely defpifed. In a regular action fo foon as the enemy's infantry are perceived to lofe ground, or ballancing between refiftance and retreat, the cavalry of the referve fhould inftantly pafs through the firft line of infantry ; and the firft fquadron that is formed, fhould charge forward with all the vigour poffible, without waiting for the others, who ought alfo to make all poffible difpatch to follow and fupport them, for every moment is precious on fuch an occafion.

It is then that the greateft havoc is made amongft the enemy's infantry ; the foldiers throwing themfelves upon the ground pretending to be dead, to efcape being fabred ; and it frequently happens that they will fuffer themfelves to be ftripped and plundered, and left naked in the depth of winter, in the open field, without giving the leaft figns of life, an inftance of which particularly occured at Catholic Hennerfdorf, in Saxony, in 1745.

From the above remarks, it is apparent that the moft effential of the operations of cavalry confifts in the vivacity and precifion of its movements, and thefe are advantages which the Pruffians poffefs in a fuperior degree, becaufe they are continually practifed to it, both in camps of inftruction, in time of peace, and in the more important operations of war, in actual fervice.

The

The march in line ought always to be prefered when practicable in the prefence of an enemy ; any number of fquadrons can then change their point of attack, or manœuvre with the fame facility as a fingle regiment, and keep an enemy who depends upon the goodnefs of his pofition, and has not the fame confidence in the precifion of his own manœuvres, in the greateft fufpence and uncertainty, until the moment that the troops fuddenly move forward to the charge, upon the moft favourable point for them, and where perhaps leaft expected by the enemy.

The cavalry of the corps de referve ought to be pofted as near the fecond line as poffible, or fome fquadrons in the intervals, this will enable them to arrive in time to fupport the infantry of the firft line, on any point required, or in which the enemy's cavalry might have made an impreffion.

Or if the cavalry of the referve fhould be required to advance upon the enemy's infantry, in a critical moment of confufion, or hefitation, this corps, by fuch difpofition, will be at hand inftantly to perform that fervice, and feize, with rapidity, that decifive advantage the inftant it offers. It ought however to be obferved, that the abovementioned nature of troops fhould not be pofted in fuch fituations as to be unneceffarily expofed to the fire of the enemy's artillery.

The infantry of the referve is rarely of any confiderable fervice in an open and plain country, becaufe it cannot move with fufficient expedition, to any point upon which the greateft efforts of the enemy might be directed, or to oppofe their progrefs where they may have been fo fuccefsful as to penetrate.

The

The only fervice which can be expected from them in fuch fituations, is to cover the retreat in cafe it becomes neceffary; and even that is not always to be depended upon: for if the enemy's cavalry fhould follow clofe upon the rear of thofe who retire in diforder, it cannot always avoid being hurried away with them. It would be almoft impoffible for the infantry of the referve to make any effectual oppofition in fuch confufion, where they even to wait for the victorious enemy, becaufe it would be impoffible to make ufe of their fire in fuch a multitude, or even to diftinguifh the enemy, until they were within reach of their fabres; it is therefore a very bad crifis, when at the clofe of an action it is neceffary to have recourfe to the battalions of the referve to cover the retreat.

It fhould be remarked, that when the wing of an enemy's cavalry has been routed, they ought, by proper manœuvres, to be always thrown upon the lines of their own infantry; it was a fimilar manœuvre which caufed that complete and total deroute at Rofback.

CHAP.

C H A P.   IX.

Of the Movements of Cavalry, in oblique Line.

THE attack in oblique line, or as it was formerly called, in echarpe, is the moſt formidable of all the orders of attack, and ought never to be omitted, when practicable, as it is the moſt difficult of all others for an enemy to reſiſt, or evade.

An officer who perceives the enemy forming an oblique line, with an intent of attacking him in his poſition, cannot make uſe of a more effectual manœuvre to counteract it, than by inſtantly moving forward to attack him, before he has completed his diſpoſition; this manœuvre, by reducing him from, the offenſive to the defenſive, muſt totally derange his plan of operations, will oblige him ſuddenly to form a new order of attack, totally different from his original intention, which cannot fail of being defective, as it is the effect of precipitation, and almoſt ſurpriſe. Such decided movements as that above propoſed, by deranging the preconcerted plans of an enemy's attack, in the moment of their execution, are capable of producing very great and advantageous effects.

If the Auſtrians had followed this ſyſtem at Leuthen, as they might have done, by advancing upon the heads of the Pruſſian columns, ſo

Y   ſoon

foon as they made their appearance, that day would have been con-
cluded with a fuccefs totally different.

It is therefore very important to conceal, as much as poffible, the
difpofitions preparatory to an attack, in oblique line, from the enemy
a corps of light cavalry fhould be thrown forward, to prevent him
from reconnoitring the previous movements, and to mafk, by every
means in their power, the difpofition of the line, until it is ready to
move forward to the attack; or feigned demonftrations might be
made, in various directions, to deceive and confound the enemy, and
prevent his having any diftinct conception of the real attack, until it is too
late to avoid, or counteract it.

The ufual manner of performing this manœuvre, is for the divifions
to move forward upon the given alignement: and then, by wheeling
up, they are at once formed in oblique line upon the enemy's flank, as
has been mentioned in the defcription of the battle of Leuthen.

Or an oblique line might be formed by the following movements:
After the enemy's Huffars have been driven in from their advanced
pofts upon their lines, to prevent their reconnoitring the difpofition,
a point of view muft be given to the officer upon the flank, to which
the oblique is to be formed, upon which the flank file of his troop
muft direct the head of his horfe: the other troopers muft clofe up
to that flank, and lay the heads of their horfes againft the knee of the
trooper, on the flank towards which they are to oblique: this is called
head to boot; by this means, a regiment of five fquadrons, moving
500 paces forward, might gain 100 paces to the right or left, and the
oppofite flank will be 50 paces retired: and the line will be formed in

perfect

Plate 24.*

Fifth Manœuvre

perfect oblique, by only turning the horfes head a little towards the oppofite hand.

This is a very fafe manœuvre to perform in the prefence of an enemy, as the line is inftantly formed, either by moving ftraight forward, or by inclining the horfes head to the oppofite flank; and it ought always to be made ufe of to deploy into line. Marching into the alignment by divifions, in the prefence of an enemy, is fubject to great caution, as the divifions upon the wheel to form line, prefent fo many flanks, which an active light cavalry would not fail taking the advantage of. Another advantage of forming the oblique upon an enemy's flank, by the above movement, is the difficulty of its being difcerned by the enemy : for it is not eafy to diftinguifh at a diftance, whether cavalry formed in line is correctly parallel, or whether it inclines gradually to one flank or the other, or even if it is in motion, until the ftandards are perceived in the pofition for the charge, and the fquadrons formed to their proper front ; whereas if the fquadrons were to break into divifions, the intention of that movement could not be an inftant concealed from them.

This method of performing the oblique manœuvre renders it very eafy and correct, and is very important to be particularly recollected.

By this movement alfo a wing of an army might change its pofition, and march upon any new point of appui, without deranging its proper front : but then the retired flank muft move up and drefs with that they have been marching upon ; this is done fucceffively by files, which is at the fame time correct and expeditious.

Another

Another fpecies of oblique, made ufe of by the Pruffians, is to reinforce that wing of the army which is oppofed to the weakeft of the
enemy's, to make the whole effort with that reinforced wing, and to
regulate the obliquity of the reft of the line, by its progrefs; the wing
which is not reinforced muft be kept retired, and refufe the action, the
reft of the line fucceffively engages, as the reinforced wing advances.
This manœuvre was performed at Leuthen, with the greateft preciffion
and fuccefs, and feveral officers prefent could not comprehend how it happened, that although at the beginning of the action we were upon the
left flank of the Auftrian army; and with a fmall front, we fhould neverthelefs outflank their right at the clofe of the action.

Puifegur, in his remarks upon the battle of Nordlingen, treats perfectly of the oblique, (this is his mafter piece) and it was agreeable to
his principles that the King of Pruffia manœuvered, at the battle of
Colin, where, if it had not been for the miftakes of Prince M————,
of D————, and of General M————, we fhould have had all the
fuccefs which the excellent difpofitions of the King fo much merited,
fince the principal difficulties were already conquered, by carrying the
heights, upon which the Auftrian's right was formed, and that almoft
without lofs.

CHAP.

C H A P. X.

Of Cavalry, and Infantry, combined in Corps,

IT has already been obferved, that the incorporated combination of
cavalry, and infantry, was very proper, and even neceffary, againft the
Turks, becaufe their infantry, not being regularly formed, nor having
any bayonets, and re-charging their fire-arms very flowly, cavalry
has nothing to apprehend from them, (and might advance with their
pipes in their mouths) but notwithftanding, any thing which might be
afferted to the contrary, fuch mixed difpofitions againft regular troops,
formed upon principles of European taĉticks, would be extremely de-
fećtive, and thedefeat of thofe troops, by whom it is adopted, muft be
the inevitable confequence: for in a line of troops thus compofed,
the cavalry would be obliged to march with the fame pace as the in-
infantry, and to halt when they did; this alone is fufficient to deprive
them of their greateft advantage, which is, rapidity. Let it be likewife
confidered, by advancing thus flowly againft a line of infantry, what repeated difcharges they muft receive, without being in any manner
enabled to take their revenge; the enemy's infantry and artillery,
which happens to be oppofed to them, will be perfećtly at their eafe,
and enabled deliberately to take their aim, and re-load, without inter-

Z   ruption;

ruption ; and the deſtruction of the cavalry would be certain, before it arrived within 200 paces of the enemy's line.

Should the cavalry determine to charge forwards, ſword in hand, the manœuvre which is proper for them, they muſt renounce the protection which it is pretended they receive from their infantry, and would not be formed in proper order for the charge of regular infantry, in an advantageous poſition, and which has not been in the leaſt deranged by any attack : and ſhould they be repulſed, the troopers are in too much haſte to get from under the enemy's fire, to examine whether they retire by the ſame way they came, or not : but commonly diſperſe in all directions, and would riſk the involving their infantry in the ſame diſorder, whilſt the enemy would not fail to keep up a briſk and heavy fire, which would be the more deſtructive, from the impoſſibility of returning it.

Cavalry incorporated with infantry in line, looſes all the advantage of its activity and motion : for if it leaves its poſition in the line, the whole order of battle is deranged, whilſt that of the enemy, formed in the uſual manner, in the rear of their infantry, or on the wings, is at liberty to move in every direction to ſeize every advantage, and to attack at pleaſure, either the flank or rear. Should the incorporated cavalry quit the line to charge, the battalions would be left with too large intervals, which the enemy would not fail to enter, and roll them up by the flanks : and ſhould the cavalry wait in line the charge of the enemy, their defeat is certain, as no cavalry at reſt can ſuſtain the ſhock of one in motion, and the battalions would alſo be ſubject to the ſame inconvenience as in the former caſe.

At

At a time when there were but few fire-arms, particularly cannon, when cavalry marched up to the attack at a walk, or at moft at a trot; this combination might have been practicable, or even ufeful, as it is at this time againft irregular troops, but in any other cafe it is very dangerous, and fubjects the troops who adopt it to a certainty of being defeated, and almoft anihilated, without even a chance of making an honourable refiftance: Thofe two natures of troops thus mixed, embarrafs, inftead of protecting each other, the effence of the one being the fword, combined with the rapidity of its movement: and the other, in the quantity and direction of its fire, the fteady firmnefs of its movements, as well as precifion and order.

It is difficult to comprehend what is related by fome of the old military authors, that in the midft of an action, the cavaliers alight to fight fword in hand: this appears romantic, at leaft in our time no perfon will be eafily prevailed upon to imitate their example.

CHAP.

C H A P. XI.

Of the Service proper to Cavalry.

AGREEABLE to the inftitution of this nature of troops, the heavy cavalry, or thofe mounted upon large horfes, and armed for the defenfive, (fuch as curiafliers) ought to ferve in the firft line of the order of battle, and for this fervice they are generally referved, being rarely employed elfewhere ; the height and weight of both man and horfe, give a decided fuperiority in the charge, fuppofing it to be fimply given ftraight forward, fquadron againft fquadron, with equal impetuofity: In a courfe of 600 paces, a good German horfe, in condition, will get before a Polifh, Tartar, or other horfe of that defcription : but if the courfe is continued to a greater diftance, the latter will regain its ground, leave the other behind, and contiue in wind for a much longer time : and fhould the heavy horfe be forced a little beyond his wind, he becomes infenfible to the bit and fpur, and loofes all his activity, which is the reafon that cuiraffiers are never employed on any other occafion than a regular battle. The poft of the dragoons is regularly in the fecond line, except when there is a deficiency of cuiraffiers, or other heavy cavalry, for the firft. The Auftrians have formerly, on fome occafions, placed a regiment of dragoons on each wing of cavalry, even in the firft line, and this they feemed to do, without any good reafon, or neceffity, and when they had cuiraffiers enough to place fome in the fecond line.

A

A line of troops certainly ought not to be weaker on its flanks than in the centre, nor the charge of lefs effect or weight; if by this difpofition the Auftrians intended that the dragoons fhould be at hand to gain the enemy's flank, thofe dragoons were as little proper for that, as the cuiraffiers, their horfes being equally heavy; nor is this the moft advantageous difpofition for that purpofe, as has been already mentioned.

Huffars are placed upon the extremities of wings; and in the re-ferve, they are alfo employed in fkirmifhing, more than any other nature of troops; dragoons are the medium between heavy cavalry and that which is properly called light, and they act occafionally with one or the other.

The Pruffian Huffars have fhewn that they are equally capable of every nature of fervice. In regular battles they have rendered the fer-vice of cuiraffiers; they never hefitated to attack in clofe fquadron, whatever they have met with, which was never known before them, to have been done by the Huffars of any other nation; it being the general opinion, and even Huffars themfelves, in thofe fervices, do not conceive that nature of arm to be proper to act in line, nor do they fcarcely ever make their appearance during an action, which could originate only from the antient prejudice that the goodnefs of cavalry confifted, exclufively in the height of the man and horfe. The cavaliers, however, of Guftavus Adolphus, and Charles XII. were never mounted upon any other than Swedifh, Finland, or Livonian nags, (or poneys) and neverthelefs performed wonders.

A a

According

According to the maxims of the Count de Saxe, the cuiraffiers ought never to quit the camp, and of courfe never fee the enemy, except on the day of battle : The King of Pruffia, with more reafon, thought differently. No cavalry can be good that has not frequent occafions to exercife their addrefs and courage againft the enemy : for which reafon, the cuiraffiers, as well as others, ought frequently to be commanded on detachments, provided it is not at too great a diftance, nor fo frequent as to harrafs the horfes ; they fhould be allowed to fkirmifh often with the enemy's, detachments, which will render them quick, bold, and dexterous in the management of their horfes, and their arms. Auftrians fometimes have incorporated dragoons, and cuiraffiers, in the fame detachment, by alternate files : This has a difagreeable effect upon the eye, befides which, it is much better that each troop fhould act diftinctly under the command of their own officers, whom they have been accuftomed to obey, and who is acquainted with the peculiar routine, and cuftoms, of their refpective regiments, as the nature and fervice of which are fo widely different. Sometimes the Auftrians have thus incorporated German cuiraffiers, with Flemifh dragoons, who could not fpeak the fame language, nor underftand each other. The King of Pruffia never permitted this kind of combination.

CHAP.

C H A P. XII.

Particular Observations relative to Cavalry.

THERE are some few situations in which regular cavalry must act contrary to what is allowed to be the essence of that arm; as for instance: in presence of a numerous corps of irregular light cavalry, as Hussars, Tartars, &c. it would be at the risk of their total anihilation, to charge forward with such impetuosity as to risk being in disorder, or the squadron dispersed for a moment: But the arm, which in such instance might be used with the greatest advantage, and effect, is the carbine, and pistols, as such troops always stand in the greatest awe of them, and keep at a very respectable distance. The greatest care should be taken never to charge troops of that description, in line, or close squadron, except when they should happen to be in such a position as to be incapable of avoiding it by dispersing, as in a defilé, or other enclosed situation.

An army moving forward towards the enemy, usually meets with several detachments of his troops upon the line of march, some of whom will attempt to pass between the columns to throw them into disorder; to obviate this inconvenience, detachments of Hussars are commonly posted at the head of each of the columns, and to those are joined some chasseurs, or markimen, with rifle carbines, and ammusfetes, who are, on no account, to separate themselves from them.

A few

A few Huſſars are likewiſe detached to ſerve as flankers : theſe muſt diſperſe and extend themſelves to reconnoitre and examine every thing on the right and left, and between the columns ; and ſome Huſſars are likewiſe to be poſted in the rear of the chaſſeurs for their protection, and always to remain within 150 paces of them ; this diſpoſition will effectually prevent the enemy's detachments from inſinuating them-ſelves between the columns, and throwing them into confuſion, by firing upon the diviſions on their march, as it has frequently happened where ſuch precautions have been neglected.

If the line of march of the columns is at any conſiderable diſtance from each other, ſome ſquadrons muſt march in the intermediate ſpace, to preſerve a free communication, as well as to prevent parties of the enemy from taking the advantage of their ſeparation. In a plain country theſe ſquadrons ſhould not march at the height of the heads of the column, but retire as it were in echiquier, by which diſpoſition they will at the ſame time ſecure their own flanks, and be enabled to fall upon thoſe of the enemy who might attempt to attack the flanks of the diviſions, which form the heads of the columns. See the plan.

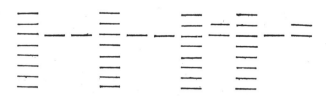

It was in this order the Pruſſians marched, at Frankfort, the enemy's coſſacks ſtuck to the Huſſars at the heads of the columns, like ſwarms of flies, but the King ordered the Huſſars to march in ſquadrons, as cloſe as cuiraſſiers. When ſquadrons preſerve this compact formation, ſuch

troops

troops muſt of neceſſity give place ; on thoſe occaſions chaſſeurs are of the greateſt importance, becauſe all the eaſtern and light cavalry in general, keep at a reſpectable diſtance from the range of their carbines. It is certain, that Huſſars will ſometimes keep up a ſcattered fire for a whole day, with very little effect, this is however frequently unavoidable, particularly in harraſſing or being harraſſed, &c. the flankers muſt, in this caſe, be detached, to keep the enemy at a diſtance, who would otherwiſe fire upon the body of the detachment, and incommode it very much : for it is much eaſier to touch a ſquadron, than a ſingle Huſſar in continual motion; in this, Huſſars have great advantage over heavy cavalry, particularly when they have not been practiſed to this kind of ſervice. In a march of ten German miles, ſuppoſing it to be commenced with equal numbers, the Huſſars would certainly be the victors. In the open country they would very much harraſs and diſhearten heavy cavalry by continual ſkirmiſhing, and hanging upon their flanks and rear, which would be very much increaſed, if they ſhould be provoked to charge, even if they ſhould be ſo fortunate as not to be in diſorder after it : but in ſuch a length of march, there muſt at laſt be ſome defilé, or other obſtacle, which would oblige this heavy cavalry, already much fatigued, to break off; and this is the moment, for the light troops to act with the greateſt vigour, and by continual preſſing upon them in ſuch ſituations, in which they can neither prevent being attacked, nor take their revenge, they will at length loſe confidence; and the inſtant they either charge or diſperſe, they are equally certain of being vanquiſhed.

To remedy this diſadvantage the King of Pruſſia directed all his cuiraſſiers to be practiſed to the Huſſar exerciſes, which was certainly

B b

ſo

fo far ufeful : but their horfes are not proper for fuch light and active fervice.

Seydlitz, whofe regiment ought, for the ufeful, to ferve as a model for all the cavalry in the univerfe; allowed, that in a march of length he fhould not be able, with his whole regiment, to refift 600 good Huffars. All heavy cavalry who lofe confidence, or difperfe, in prefence of light, is loft; if they determine, by one great effort, to extricate them-felves, at leaft for fome time: thofe retreat fwiftly, a la debandade, in all directions. If the cuiraffiers halt, and found the apell, or rally, the Huffars do the fame, and re-commence their fkirmifhing; in fhort, whe-ther they move forward, or remain upon their ground, they muft equally fuffer and be harraffed. Pruffian Huffars indeed do not always ftand upon fo much ceremony, but fall upon an arrear guard, or other corps in clofe fquadron, without hefitation, and with the greateft effect.

General Werner, with 700 Huffars, completely deftroyed the dragoons of the Arch Duke Jofeph, afterwards Emperor, by fkirmifh-ing, harraffing, and hanging upon their flanks, and rear, in the man-ner above defcribed; thofe dragoons were commanded by General Caramelli.

If during a battle, a wing of cavalry fhould be detached on fome particular fervice, to turn a flank of the enemy, to reinforce the oppo-fite wing, or any part of the line, &c. the General commanding it fhould, neverthelefs, take care to leave a few fquadrons to cover the flanks of the line, from which his wing is removed; for whatever precautions the infantry, or even artillery may take, by forming the oblong fquare, or flank firing, their pofition will be very defective,

without

without a certain proportion of cavalry. When a flank is formed by some battalions fronting outward, the few fquadrons which have been left, fhould place themfelves in the prolongation of the fecond line, by which they will be enabled to fall upon the flank of any thing which might be advifed, to attack the flank of their firft line at the fame time that the flanking battalions would attack them in front.

But if the infantry fhould not have their flanks thus clofed, the fquadrons fhould then place themfelves beyond the flanks, and oppofite to the intervals between the two lines, which will more effectually protect the flank of the firft line than if they were formed upon it.

If there were fquadrons enough to place others, at the fame time, without, and in echellon in the rear of thefe, the pofition would be yet more perfect.

It

It is a general maxim, never to leave, on any account whatever, the flanks of infantry entirely without cavalry. At Rofback, Seydlitz left only the grand guards, on the right of the lines.

If between the lines of infantry, of an army formed in order of battle, there fhould happen to be a rifing ground, trees, &c. or any thing fufficient to mafk a few fquadrons from the fight of the enemy, and not too much expofed to their fire, fuch an advantage muft not be omitted, it will be of the utmoft importance, fhould the firft line be broken, and give way; thefe frefh fquadrons, by their fudden appearance, will effectually check the advancing enemy, and by giving time to the fecond line to move forward, reftore the fuccefs of the action. On the contrary, fhould the firft line fucceed in throwing the enemy's battalions into diforder, thefe fquadrons will be ready to advance rapidly upon them, and complete their defeat.

The fpanifh dragoons, of Sagorté, performed this manœuvre, at Campo Santo, and by it, totally defeated the Auftrian and Piedmontefe cavalry, and it was this fuccefs alone which prevented the complete anihilation of the Spanifh infantry, on that day, which however fuffered very confiderably, becaufe the Duke of Artrifko, who commanded the Spanifh cavalry, purfued with the whole of his, that of the enemy, which he had juft defeated, inftead of referving fome of the fquadrons to fall upon the flanks and rear of their infantry; and by this miftake, although he fo glorioufly defeated the enemy's cavalry, he was the caufe of the lofs of the battle.

Several officers who ferved with the Spaniards, in Portugal, have declared that their cavalry is, at this time, totally unacquainted with the fervice,

that

they neglected, either through ignorance, or ill will, the moſt favourable opportunities of decided advantages ; the only point of ſervice
they ſeemed to look upon as their duty, was to remain fixed to the
ſame place, until it became their turn to retreat. The race of both
men and horſes, muſt, and have moſt furiouſly degenerated in that
country.

In an open country, an active, brave, and well diſciplined cavalry,
will frequently decide the fate of a battle, notwithſtanding the ſuperiority of the enemy's infantry, whether in number or quality, to that
of the army to which they are attached. But to this effect the infantry
muſt refuſe the action, except by a diſtant fire of artillery, and a de-
monſtration of moving forward, but without gaining too much ground,
to avoid being too cloſely engaged, or encouraging the enemy to advance, this will give time to their own cavalry to charge and overſet that
of the enemy, and throw it in confuſion upon their own infantry, which
operation being ſeconded by the infantry, with vigour, will complete
the defeat of the enemy's whole line.

C c

CHAP.

C H A P. XIII.

Of wheeling by Divisions, and by Fours.

THIS article having been already mentioned in the regimental manœuvres, I fhould not have noticed it again, had not fome perfons,
who pretend to be acquainted with the movements of cavalry, maintained that a fquadron comes more readily about by wheeling by divifions,
than by fours; this opinion can proceed only from either not having confidered the fubject, or that they are not what they imagine themfelves to be.

Firft. The operation of coming to the right about, is performed in a
much fhorter time by fours, than by divifions.

Second. The horfes hardly move from off their own ground, and the
order of the fquadron is not deranged by fours, as it is by divifions.

Third. It can be performed on any ground, without fpare fpace,
or intervals, either between the fquadrons or upon the flanks, as the
two horfes on the right, and thofe on the left move into and occupy
each others ground exactly ; by the four moving upon their centre, the
two right hand troopers retiring their horfes a little, whilft the other two
advance with theirs, until each fall into the others places.

Fourth.

Fourth. The fquadrons occupy exactly the fame ground, after having come to the right about, as they did before; whereas by the fame manœuvre, by divifions, every fquadron, and of courfe the whole line, muft gain ground a whole divifions length to the right.

Fifth. Becaufe by wheeling by divifions the order of the fquadron is wholly deranged, the flank becomes almoft in the centre.

Sixth. Becaufe a line en murialle cannot wheel by divifions without the right hand divifions moving out of the line, to make room for the others to wheel into, which is a dangerous operation, very irregular, and in many cafes impracticable: whereas by fours it may be performed with regularity and precifion, in any fituation.

The Pruffian reglement commands the performance of this manœuvre by fours, explains the manner in which it ought to be executed, and the aids to be employed.

As this manœuvre has been for time immemorial practifed in the German armies, it is furprifing that Monf. de Puifegur fhould have had no knowledge of it; his pretended Wieder Zurück, has not been practifed this century.

CHAP.

C H A P. XIV.

Of the Caracol, or wheeling the Regiment in Line.

THE King of Pruffia formerly, in all his reviews, made ten, or even as many as twenty fquadrons, wheel together in line, fometimes en muraille, at others with intervals of ten or twelve paces. Sometimes a regiment wheeled upon its centre; notwithstanding this authority, and that of Monf. Puifegur, who very earneftly recommends it, and was then in fafhion; this manœuvre has, fince that time, been univerfally exploded.

When this manœuvre is to be performed in line, or barrier, as it is fometimes called, one wing keeps the rein in hand, whilft the other turns full fpeed, as in the wheeling a fingle fquadron, which is neverthelefs very flow and difficult to perform; at prefent it is done with much more expedition and facility: the pivot fquadron wheels at once, without attending at all to the others, and thofe move rapidly forwards, to fall into their places upon each others flank in fucceffion, as they arrive into the alignement, by moving on the fhorteft line, and without forming any part of a circle. If they are wheeling to the right, they have no occafion to turn their eyes to the left, as when wheeling in line, or fquadron, but only to look to the pivot; and to drefs into

the

the alignement by the preceding fquadron. This manœuvre has the advantage of a certain number of fquadrons being always ready for action, and thofe continually increafing until the whole has wheeled, and are in no rifk of lofing their intervals.

The half wheel, is correctly performed by the counter march by divifions, which has none of the inconveniences of the wheeling en barriere, or line.

If a line of troops, or a regiment is to wheel or change front to the rear, the right hand fquadron wheels to the right about, or half wheel, all the others to the right, quarter wheel; and march in the rear of it, and wheel up into line, as they arrive in fucceffion upon the left flank of each other.

D d

CHAP.

C H A P. XV.

Of Rallying.

WHETHER cavalry has been fuccefsful, or the contrary, it is always more or lefs in diforder after a charge, and it is neceffary to rally the fquadrons as quickly as poffible, by founding the appel; this fhould be frequently practifed at exercife, and thofe troopers who do not fall in with brifknefs and difpatch, fhould be punifhed. There are two methods of performing this manœuvre, the firft and moft common is, when the commanding officer, after having ordered the appel to be founded, remains in the rear; and the troopers, fo foon as they hear it, return and form upon the ftandard in his front; this method is proper only when a few files have been detached from the flanks, to purfue, and fkirmifh with the enemy. But when the whole are to be rallied after a charge, the commanding officers of the fquadrons, with the trumpeters, and ftandards, fhould continue to move forward, and gain the foremoft of the fcattered troopers. So foon as a few files are collected, they fhould continue to advance flowly, by which means the others will have much greater facility in joining them, and to fall into their places in the ranks, than if the troop remained upon its own ground in the rear, to wait for them to return to the ftandard; which would likewife very much retard the purfuit, and give the enemy time to reconnoitre, and rally in his turn; befides many other very ferious difadvantages.

The

The King of Pruffia firft introduced the practice of rallying, advancing; the other method was formerly practifed in his army, as well as in all others in Europe, but the fuperiority of that was immediately perceived, and has fince been very frequently confirmed by experience.

On the day of Penticoft, in the year 1745, a fmart action took place at Llandfhut, in Silefia, between the Pruffians and the Auftrians, to oblige the latter to evacuate that province ; the regiment to which the author belonged, was in the fecond line of the Pruffian army : in approaching the village of Riechennerfdorf, they perceived Colonel Soldau, in the firft line, permitting the Auftrian Huffars to file off quietly by the village, and retire : Seydlitz, Malakoufky, and the author of this effay, to whom this deliberate conduct was not agreeable, paffed through the intervals of the firft line, formed, and made a fuccefsful charge, purfued the enemy through the village, and were very near furrounding ten fquadrons of Huffars with Prince Efterhazy, who commanded them, at the defilé of Faulbrük, which we were very well acquainted with ; when Soldau perceiving that one of his fquadrons had joined us, founded the appel, or rally : this caufed the whole of the Huffars to retire in diforder, and by this miftake, the enemy not only found themfelves in fecurity, but faced about, and followed them to the village, and the author himfelf was very near being taken : whereas, had the Huffars been practifed to rally in advancing, this check would not have happened.

At

However, the files firſt formed ſhould always move ſlowly forward, to facilitate the falling in of the others to their places as they arrive.

The King of Pruſſia payed great attention to the appel, and if any regiment neglected, or were imperfect in it, he expreſſed the greateſt diſſatisfaction.

C H A P. XVI.

Various Observations upon Cavalry.

WELL diſciplined cavalry ſhould be formed to every kind of uſeful manœuvre, which is practicable in preſence of an enemy, even if it ſhould be required only once in ten campaigns.

It is very important that they ſhould be particularly exerciſed to all the operations of cavalry, in an arrear guard. The Pruſſian Huſſars have rarely attacked a rear guard, without ſucceſs : but their enemies have never acted with ſimilar energy, if we except General Tottleben, when he defeated that of General Goltz, near Weitzeig. If the Auſtrians had acted with more vigour, againſt the late Prince of Pruſſia, in the long retreat from Böhmiſch Lippa, to Zittau, and Boutzen; his army muſt have ſuffered much more conſiderably; particularly when

it

it decamped from Zittau. The author, who commanded the rear guard, during the whole of that march, was much furprifed at being fo little harraffed, and loft but very few troops by the operations of the enemy, but the mifconduct of fome of the general officers, caufed a greater lofs by defertion, than would have been fuftained by the lofs of a moderate battle.

In any country which is not entirely mountainous, a good corps of active cavalry, commanded by experienced officers, cannot fail to defeat an enemy's arrear guard: fooner or later a favourable opportunity, if carefully attended to, muft prefent itfelf to ftrike a decifive blow. General Seydlitz, and the author, at that time both Majors, had this advantage near Zittau, by which they defeated the rear guard, commanded by Count Burghaufen, in 1745. Another time the author had a like advantage over an arrear guard, commanded by General Brown, on the march, to fuccour the Saxons, near Schandau; he had not then with him, more than 400 Huffars, and both times attacked the enemy's infantry in the plain.

Defenfive operations are always difadvantageous to cavalry; however well they may do their duty, manœuvring in retreat, they cannot avoid fooner or later meeting with a confiderable check, if not a defeat; the carbine is the proper arm of defence, but they will not be able with it, entirely to reftrain for any confiderable time, any but fuch irregular light cavalry, as Tartars, and troops of that defcription; it is for this reafon that an arrear guard fhould always be compofed of infantry with field pieces, and chaffeurs, as well as dragoons, huffars, &c. that each nature of troops may reciprocally fupport the other.

The

The cavalry will fupport the infantry and artillery in the plain, and the infantry cover the retreat of the cavalry, in defilés, or mountainous paffes, and the chaffeurs keep the enemy's flankers at a diftance, in both places. A rear guard thus compofed, with proper meafures, will run as little rifk of being harraffed in their retreat, as the nature of the operation will admit; except, by fome grofs overfight, they fhould allow themfelves to be feparated from the columns, and taken in the rear or flank. It is neceffary to act with great precaution in mountains and woods, and other enclofed countries. It once happened that a detachment, commanded by the author, was very much harraffed by the enemy's croats on its march near Königfgratz, in an enclofed country, very much interfected by deep ditches: but the detachment moved into the plain where the croats had the imprudence likewife to follow; the fquadron faced fuddenly to the right about, and in a moment fabred the greateft number of them in prefence of the King.

It is certain that no cavalry unfupported by infantry, can be fure of making a good retreat of any length, in prefence of other cavalry who do their duty.

All irregular cavalry have a great dread of fire-arms, and it is advantageous not to undeceive that of the enemy, with regard to the fmallnefs of the effect of it from cavalry; therefore when they advance with their lances in the air, emitting their ufual barbarous fcreams, they fhould be received with firmnefs, and the front rank level at them with the carbine, which when they perceive, before they arrive within fixty paces diftance, they never fail to retreat with more precipitation than they advanced: a few fhot only, from fome good markfmen, fhould then be fired after them: for if a whole rank was to fire, and none of them be
touched,

touched, which is not unlikely to happen, inftead of confirming their refpect for the fire of the carbine, it would fhew them its weaknefs when made ufe of by cavalry, and their own advantage, which would make them more enterprifing for the future ; the Pruffians, by being too lavifh of their carbine firing, emboldened the coffacks to a contempt of that fire, which at the commencement of the war they had dreaded very much; but it is certain that this muft have happened fooner or later, from the difproportion of numbers of the Pruffian Huffars to the Ruffian light cavalry, of every fpecies, which they had to oppofe.

The Pruffian Huffars were nearly exhaufted with fatigue ; they were in continual motion from one enemy to another, in fummer and winter, without ever being in quarters, or cantonments, which is fo neceffary for the re-eftablifhment of troops, particularly cavalry ; every campaign the regiments were obliged to be almoft renewed : no wonder then if the Huffars had frequently recourfe to the carbine, of which the enemy's coffacks ftood fo much in awe, and by that means, on many occafions, to leffen the fatigues of the fervice.

A Peafant, or other recruit, was enlifted, cloathed, and exercifed on foot, during eight days; his horfe was then given him, and he was immediately fent to join the regiment in actual fervice againft the enemy. Without the affiftance of our own coffacks, it would, after all, have been impoffible for us to refift.

CHAP.

C H A P. XVII.

Of the Points of Alignement, of View, and of Appui.

THE point of alignement is any diftant objeʄt ferving as a direʄtion, upon which to form the regiments into line, in order of battle; there is ufually one chofen in the direʄtion of each flank, remarkable buildings, woods, fteeples, villages, &c. are proper objeʄts for this purpofe.

Points of appui are fituations chofen for the pofition of wings of an army, by which they are covered, fupported, and proteʄted; fometimes only one wing has this advantage, but if they fhould be given to both, and more troops than fufficient to occupy the fpace between them in the firft line, fome battalions fhould be formed in interline: but if on the contrary, the points of appui fhould be at fuch diftance from each other as to require more troops to occupy the fpace between them, the intervals muft be clofed up by fome battalions from the fecond line, and thofe replaced from the corps de referve; but fhould the army advance, and quit the points of appui, the lines, and corps de referve, fhould refume their former difpofition, if the ground and other circumftances will admit.

Points

Points of appui are therefore any objects which tend to strengthen the wings appuied upon them, and if perfect, to render them inattackable by the enemy; such as impassable marshes, or swampy grounds, lakes, and large pieces of water, deep ravines, and steep precipieces, heights, &c. with works and cannon upon them, fortified villages, woods with abbatis in them, a military eye will discover some of these objects, and apply them with advantage, in almost every situation.

The points of view are objects selected in a line perpendicular to the front, and to serve as points of direction, upon which the line is to advance, to enable it to move in parallel lines directly forward without gaining ground to the right or left, or obliquing the line, which would expose one of the flanks to the enemy's fire.

Great accuracy is required in the selection of these points, that they may be chosen correctly perpendicular, and at proper distances from each other, that the battalions, or brigades, might not cross upon, or separate from each other upon converging or diverging lines.

Points of view are likewise made use of for the march of the army, in columns, towards the enemy, which requires equal accuracy, that they might preserve their proper distances for the battalions to deploy into line, and reform the order of battle.

The interline is a line of troops formed between the two lines of the army, but generally nearest to the first; from whence they are taken for want of space, or other reasons, and into which they reform so soon as those reasons cease.

F f

When

When mention is made of an army, in order of battle, it is said the right or left wing of cavalry ; and simply the right or left of infantry.

The antient idea that it was advantageous for an army to remain in a permanent position, and receive the attack, where villages happened to be situated in its front, is at present entirely exploded. Such villages were formerly fortified in haste, filled with artillery and infantry, and obstinately defended, and supported to the last extremity by the whole army; and the village taken, the battle was lost: Neerwinde furnishes an example. At Ramalies, so soon as the French infantry was dislodged from the village, the cavalry could act, and the affair was soon decided. At Keselsdorf, the Saxons not being able to re-enter it, the same thing ensued. In the war, in Flanders, the battles of the Count de Saxe were won by taking villages, which whether built of brick, or wood, would at present be no longer tenable, howitzer shells would soon set them on fire, or the great number of cannons would soon batter them, and dislodge the most resolute troops.

The affair at Leuthen, might seem to militate against this assertion, as we lost more men in the attack of it, than in all the rest of the action : but that is not the case, the Austrians entered that village during the action, and it was not placed in their front, but between the two lines ; it was, I believe, their reserve, which had moved from the right towards the left, and entered just as our troops approached it, and what very much increased the strength of it was, an elevated church yard, with thick walls, like a kind of citadel, and very strong. However, if we had waited for the heavy cannon, which were coming from the right, instead of persisting in carrying it by assault, we should have had it at a very cheap rate, notwithstanding the resolution with which it

was

was defended. At prefent villages are more avoided than fearched after, becaufe it is very difadvantageous for an army to be embarraffed in its movements; they are generally fet on fire, to prevent the enemy taking any advantage of them.

When armies had but few cannon, and no howitzers, the attack of a village was an important and difficult operation.

When a village happens to be fituated in fo ftrong a pofition as that of Berghen, near Frankfort, it might however well merit being defended and fupported. When that had been well reconnoitred by Prince Ferdinand, I am affured he determined not to attack it, but was engaged in that action, by the imprudent courage of Prince Ifembourg, who was killed in the attack.

It is commonly at the choice of the General, either to force the village with his artillery alone, or to mafk it with a few troops, and direct his attacks elfewhere: fhould the remainder of their army be defeated, or obliged to retreat, it will be next to impoffible for thofe in the village to extricate themfelves, and will be obliged to furrender, without having performed the leaft fervice; this happened to the French, at Höckftädt.

A General who would at prefent embarrafs his movements, by fupporting a village in his front, would almoft certainly enfure his own defeat, and the lofs of the troops pofted in it.

The King of Pruffia, whofe fyftem was always to attack, would not fuffer ground to be broken in front of his pofitions; it was with great difficulty

ficulty that he would permit a few flefhes to be thrown up to cover the guards of infantry.

He frequently repeated that no good was to be expected from that army which was cramped it its movements, as it would prevent them from manœuvring, or taking advantage of the miftakes or faults of the enemy.

What are we to think of thofe battles were a whole army fally out of an intricate pofition, by one fingle avenue, and fall unexpectly upon that which is marching to attack it; but that they are of a piece with thofe immenfe towers of ftone which were advanced upon rollers, to the attack of fortified places; and with thofe corbeaux, or crows of iron, which caught the veffels up out of the fea, and fhook them to pieces; or the balliftas which projected whole rocks with as much precifion as we throw fhells from mortars.

There are fome occafions in which it is neceffary for an army to intrench; particularly when by the great fuperiority of numbers of the enemy, it is reduced to the defenfive: as the King of Pruffia was before Schweidnitz, when it was invefted by the combined armies of Auftria, and Ruffia. In fuch cafes the cavalry is always encamped in the rear of the infantry, covered as much as poffible from the fire of the enemy's artillery, and if time will admit, large epaulments thrown up in their front, with wide intervals, that the fquadrons might be enabled to advance freely through them.

The cavalry might even be allowed to difmount, if it fhould happen to be intrenched in the rear of a pofition fubject to be brifkly cannonaded,

for

for nothing difheartens troops fo much as to be expofed to fuffer without being enabled to take their revenge, or being of any fervice.

Active light cavalry, though they might not be able to fupport the charge of compact fquadrons of heavy horfe, yet they will not be in danger of fuffering confiderably by being defeated by them; the light-nefs and activity of their horfes will enable them to difperfe in all directions with fuch rapidity, that the heavy fquadrons might as well purfue a flight of fparrows, as fuch alert and active horfe; and with the fame brifknefs and facility, they will be enabled fuddenly to rally; and by continually hovering round them, fooner or later find an opportunity to take there revenge; whereas heavy cavalry, in fimilar circumftances, or once feparated and difperfed, are in the greateft danger of being totally deftroyed.

The attempt to rally routed cavalry, whilft purfued clofe by the ene-my, is generally found to be fruitlefs; every one cries halt, but no one ceafes to fly; and indeed thofe who in fuch circumftances fhould have courage enough to wait for the enemy, would only be the vic-tims of their temerity; therefore before it is attempted to rally routed cavalry, they fhould be allowed to gain a confiderable diftance from the enemy, which they would foon do, for the enemy advancing in re-gular order, cannot move with fo much fpeed.

The moft diftant troopers fhould be the firft formed, fhould it be ten or twelve files only: and then, by continuing flowly to retreat, the reft, as they arrive, will rapidly augment the troop.

G g

It

For this reafon it would be a fatal experiment to attempt to face about with the trainers, in a complete derout. When the commanding officer cannot prevent the total difperfion of his fquadron, nor fucceed in keeping any fmall number of them together, in order to cover the retreat; in thefe circumftances, it may be the duty of fuch commanding officer to be amongft the laft who difband; yet it certainly is not fo for him to be the laft trainer in the derout, but fo foon as he perceives it to be totally unavoidable, and complete, he fhould clap fpurs to his horfe, and gallop to fuch a diftance as he might think will enable him to rally, and reform a troop before the enemy will be enabled to come up with them.

Thus the moft diftant being firft rallied, and continue to move flowly, the whole will, in a very fhort time, be regularly reformed, without rifk or confufion; and be ready, by the time the enemy's fquadrons come up with them, to check the ardour of his purfuit; and even perhaps to take their revenge, and fend them in their turn to the right about, if they fhould have neglected to perform their purfuit in regular order.

CHAP.

C H A P. XVIII.

Of the Alignment of Cavalry.

IN open order, the fubaltern officers drefs to the right, or left, upon the points of alignment, with the heads of their horfes correctly upon the line; the heads of the troopers horfes of the firft rank fhould be juft clear of the croup of theirs ; the commanding officer of the fquadron pofts himfelf at four paces in front of the Subalterns line : but on the words, *clofe ranks*, the Subalterns fall back upon the flanks, or into the rear, to their pofts, except two, who remain (when there are Subalterns enough to admit of it) near the commanding officer in the front, and the one who clofes the fquadron. The commanding officer then, reins back, clofe to the front rank, in the line quitted by the Subalterns, and marks the alignment. The fuperior officers are more advanced, that they might be enabled to fee along the front of the whole line, and they drefs with each other : but thofe, except on the Parade, ought not to have any fixed poft ; the Subaltern officers on the flanks, muft be very attentive to the movements of the commanding officer of the fquadron, becaufe the alignment is always marked by him, and be careful to drefs correctly with each other, as it is upon them the fquadron is formed, when there are intervals between them ; for if there are none, or the line is formed en murialle, the whole drefs to the right, or left, or fquadron of direction, as commanded.

The

The King of Pruſſia formerly inſiſted upon the ſquadrons dreſſing
by their centres, and great confuſſion reſulted from it, ſo much, that
when the troops were manœuvring together at the reviews, the
General officers, who were anxious about the appearance and regularity
of the regiments, were obliged to evade that command, and make the
ſquadrons dreſs by the right, though the King always believed them
to dreſs by the centre.

It is more difficult for cavalry to avoid breaking the line in marching,
than infantry; theſe might march with equal pace, all the ſoldiers lift-
ing their feet at the ſame time, and ſetting them down the ſame, but
it never entered the imagination of any perſon to exact the ſame from
horſes.

Cavalry is ſometimes formed into three or four, or even more lines;
but far from being rendered of more effect, it is very much weakened
by that diſpoſition: the two firſt are the only ones which can be employed againſt the enemy, and if thoſe are defeated, they never fail to
throw the others into diſorder in their retreat; and in ſuch a maſs it is
impoſſible, in preſence of the enemy, to re-eſtabliſh order and regularity; therefore it is not unworthy of being repeated, that thirty ſquadrons in two lines, is equal to ninety in ſix; and with this advantage: that
ſhould the diſpoſition in two lines be repulſed, it is very eaſy to rally
them, which is impoſſible for the others to do, if their two firſt lines
ſhould have a ſimilar misfortune.

Marquis de Sylva recommends it as a good diſpoſition to cover the
flanks of an army with light troops: but nothing can be more ridiculous

than

than to pretend to cover the flanks of an army, which is to receive the attack, with light troops, and particularly againſt the Turks. Light troops are, no doubt, in their proper place when upon the flanks : but this is only upon the ſuppoſition of that army being the aſſailant, or that it is encamped; for in any other ſituation, the enemy's firſt attacks would be directed againſt them, and quickly make them quit their poſition, and uncover the flank of the army which they were intended to protect; as Count Saxe performed at Laufeldt, and the King of Pruſſia, at Colin ; where his firſt operation was, to diſlodge the corps commanded by Nadaſty, poſted on the right of Daun's army.

It is a deception, to imagine the flanks of an army are really covered by prolonging its front ; ſince a line, however extenſive it might be, will always have flanks; and if it is in a defenſive or permanent poſition, it will be very difficult to cover them by the means of troops; as was experienced at Leuthen. A flank cloſed with troops only, is always weak, and liable to be turned. The flank of an army, in a permanent and defenſive poſition, ought therefore always to be covered by natural obſtacles, or works. Sylva pretends that the flanks of an army, acting againſt the Turks, ſhould be covered by light cavalry, which would be an excellent breakfaſt for thoſe muſulmans, as I have had occaſion to obſerve more particularly elſewhere.

By what has been juſt mentioned, it is likewiſe eaſy to judge of the advantage the attacking army has, over that which remains in its poſition to receive the attack ; eſpecially in the preſent time, when ſuch large trains of artillery are employed.

The

The army which determines to maintain a permanent pofition, muft, at leaft, be fo ftrongly pofted, behind a river, &c. as to render it impracticable for an enemy to attack either its front or flanks, except with very great difadvantage; otherwife he will, fooner or later, find fome point where he will not fail to open himfelf a paffage, by the fuperiority of the quantity of heavy artillery, which he will always have it in his power to bring upon the point he has determined to attack; as finding it, without doubt, to be the weakeft.

C H A P.   XIX.

Remarks upon the Cavalry of the 15th and 16th Centuries, compared with the present.

IT has been obferved that it is by ferving in the light horfe, that the military fcience is moft effectually acquired, and it is, confequently, in that which an officer ought to commence his military career, as well at prefent, as in the time of Brantome, who mentions, that in his time, officers of the firft families began by ferving in the light horfe, as in a corps which was moft frequently engaged with the enemy; that author is, without doubt, the one who has left us the moft clear and diftinct memoirs of the manner of making war in his time. Paul Jove, Bifhop of Côme, throws great light upon the manner of arming and equiping

of

Plate 23.

Plate 24

Asiatick Timar.

Seydun

Plate 14

Bonnach

Plate 6

Arnaut

Plate 17.

Bostangi.

Plate 16.

of cavalry, in the 15th and 16th centuries, and as his works are not very common, I will quote a few words, which are apropos to our prefent fubject from them.

" The Gens d'Arms were armed complete, or cap-a-pied, from head to foot; the armour for the horfe was made of boiled leather. The French horfes were without ears, and without manes, and the German without tails. The offenfive arms were, the fluted lance, a long fword, a maffe d'arms, or pole-axe; each of the Gens d'Arms, or Knights, had three horfes for themfelves, a Page d'Arms, or Efquire, and two valets, all mounted, and who always fought near, or fuccoured and fupported their mafter, and were called fidefmen of fuccour, very much refembling the Spahis, Sayms, and Timars of the Turks. The lancers were upon nearly the fame footing, but each of thofe were accompanied by nine horfemen : thus, when we read, that in fuch an action there were an hundred lances, it is to be underftood there were a thoufand horfe. The great officers, Princes, and Generals, had alfo their ftandards, which were carried always before them, as it continues to be practifed among the Turks to this time.

The light horfe had likewife their defenfive armour, but not fo heavy as that of the Gens d'Arms, or Knights: their arms of offence were bows and long arrows, befides fwords, and pole-axes, with which they ufed to difpatch thofe whom the knights had unhorfed. It was in the 15th century that the Albaniens firft appeared in the Venetian armies : other nations afterwards adopted that fpecies of troops, they were called Greek cavalry; and were compofed of natives of the Levant, Greeks, Albaniens, Bofniacks, Croats, Dalmatiens, and Macedonians, or Turkifh Arnauts; they did not bear any defenfive armour, and for

arms

arms, only javelines, and cimeters, or fabres very much curved, and pole-axes, all of which are ftill in common ufe in the Turkifh cavalry; the Albaniens ferved in the field exactly fimilar to the Huffars at this prefent time; and if they had the good fortune to throw the Gens d'Arms into a little diforder, they foon made a great carnage amongft them, becaufe being hand to hand pell mell with them, thofe heavy horfemen could make no ufe of their lances, or fcarcely move themfelves. One fact occurs in the military hiftory of thofe times, which appears almoft incredible, but is neverthelefs very certain, which is, that the Swifs foot, armed fimply with pikes and halberds, attacked and defeated the Gens d'Armery, in the plain, and particularly at Novarre, where the French Gens d'Armes were almoft entirely deftroyed; this makes me doubt very much that extraordinary valour which has been fre-quently attributed to them.

In the prefent time, when a numerous train of artillery is brought into action, when all the infantry are armed with firelocks and bayonets, the Gens d'Armes dare not attack, but remain, even on a plain, inactive, in prefence of other cavalry, unlefs attacked by them.

It was Francis I. who firft adopted Arquebuffiers on horfeback: they were then, what our dragoons are now, and in very high eftimation, Monf. Brantome fpeaks thus of thofe of M. de Strozzi.

This nobleman quitted Italy, and came into France to the King, at Maroles, with the fineft company that ever was beheld; it confifted of 200 Arquebuffiers, on horfeback, the beft mounted, beft equipped, and beft appointed, that it was poffible to fee: there was not one of them who had not two horfes, which were, at that time, called

cavalins,

cavalins, which were light, handfome, and well proportioned ; their bits, and fleeves of mail, which were then worn, very ftrong ; their alfo Arque-buffes and furniture were very much gilt with gold ; and they would fre-quently run with the light horfe, and racers, to almoft enraging of them ; fometimes they made ufe of the pike, of the bourginotte, and of the coralet gilt, as occafion required : but what was moft admirable, they were all old captains, formed by ferving under the banners of that great captain John of Medicis, and had almoft all belonged to him ; infomuch, that when it was required to difmount and ferve on foot, there was no need of the word of command to form them into the order of battle ; for of themfelves they were fo well arranged, from having been fo perfectly exercifed, that no perfon could difcover any thing to find fault with."

Thus it appears thefe mounted Arquebuffiers were real dragoons, and like them of the double fervice of horfe and foot, as occafion required.

The origin of the French light horfe, was in imitation of the Vene-tian Albaniens, and like them in the middle of the 15th century, they adopted the cuirafs, which they continue to ufe to the prefent time, although the Albaniens foon experienced the inconveniency of, and rejected it. It appears by Buffy Rabutin, that the French light horfe continued to be called Albanien cavalry, until the beginning of this century ; notwithftanding they were very heavy and aukwardly accoutred, and their numbers confiderably encreafed.

I i   Philip

Philip de Commines mentions, that in his time, when the French and Venetians blocaded Verona, defended by the troops of the Emperor Maximillian; a party of Albaniens fallied from the place and fkirmifhed with the French Gens d'Arms, and that each Albanien took one of the Gens d'Arms prifoner, and led him into the town in triumph: At prefent this would not appear fo very extraordinary, as a fingle Huffar, or Coffack, has frequently taken two cuiraffiers in one day.

Huffars are a very ancient fpecies of troops: but were, till lately, little known out of Hungary; they were, what might be called according to the ancient language, light harnefs. Louis, King of France, had fome of them in his army, at the battle of Mohacs, where he loft his life, but they had defenfive armour: for the Hungarians have alfo had their Gens d'Arms, as well as other nations.

Francis I. as has been mentioned, was difgufted with his cavalry, after the battle of Novarre; conceiving them not to be of any effect, againft infantry armed with pikes, and arquebuffes; the latter, however, were but little known amongft the Swifs. He was the firft that formed legions of French infantry, in which the nobility enroled with avidity; and the cavalry was entirely neglected, and degenerated to fuch a degree, as to render it neceffary to take fome German regiments into their pay; thefe were diftinguifhed by the name of Reuters, and were always efteemed beyond their own, particularly the Weinmarienne.

The King of Pruffia has demonftrated to the world, the important advantage refulting from a proper proportion of well difciplined good cavalry, in all the operations of war; and that arm appears, in its turn, to be regaining the fuperiority.

The

The Auſtrians have never ceaſed to maintain a numerous corps of cavalry in their ſervice, the oſtenſible reaſon for which, has been the neighbourhood of the Turks ; but they do not ſeem, even to the preſent time, to have adopted that active, vigourous, and decided ſyſtem of manœuvring, ſo eſſential to the operations of cavalry ; and in which its ſuperiority and advantage principally conſiſts.

A long ſucceſſion of active campaigns very much reduces the quality, as well as the ſtrength, of regiments of infantry ; whereas in ſimilar circumſtances cavalry continue every day to improve ; unleſs whole regiments periſh, as it happened to ſeveral Pruſſian ones, at Maxen. By being frequently at blows with the enemy, they acquire a firmneſs, boldneſs, and addreſs, which cannot be by any other means infuſed into them ; and is abſolutely impoſſible to be done in time of peace : But when the infantry come to blows with the enemy, the loſs is generally ſo conſiderable, that by the end of the ſecond and third campaign, none of thoſe who made the firſt, remain ; to profit by the leſſons it afforded, or by their experience ſet an example to the young ſoldiers arrived to complete the companies : but generally by that time the regiments will conſiſt almoſt entirely of recruits.

Philip de Comines mentions, that in his time the troops ſurrounded their encampments with waggons, and other ſpare carriages ; and that it was the duty of the Gens d'Arms, to defend them on foot, as well as the breach, in caſe of an aſſault in the defence of fortified places.

F I N I S.

NOTE.

ALTHOUGH the tranflator has ftudioufly avoided touching upon any thing which related to himfelf: yet, fince this work was printed, it having been infinuated, that an officer, not regularly belonging to the cavalry, was not eligible to undertake a work fimilar to the prefent; the tranflator trufts he might, without vanity, be permitted to obferve, as one excufe amongst many others, for his prefuming to do fo, is, his having been always very partial to that nature of troops (of which the prefent tranflation is an inftance,) and having had many opportunities, (though not regularly in the cavalry) of acquiring fome little experience in it, whilft in the chief command of an army in Flanders, to which feveral excellent regiments of cavalry were attached; and having, on more than one occafion, charged with fuccefs with them; is, he prefumes, a fufficient apology for his having undertaken the tranflation of a work like the prefent, that requires no particular talents, and which he might very well have performed, had no fuch occafions occurred. Another excufe that he conceives to be equally valable is, that it has never been hitherto performed, although generally allowed by the beft cavalry officers, to be very ufeful and requifite.

Directions for placing the Plates.